Praise for *China on Strike*

"China's rise as a global economic power has been paralleled by a growing militancy among its working class. In this unfolding process, workers are gaining the confidence, experience, and tenacity to strike and to win. Censorship and political repression by the country's ruling party makes firsthand accounts of these struggles—especially in English—extremely rare. *China on Strike* fills that gap through eye-opening and compelling narratives of China's new generation of worker-militants and strike leaders. It's a must-read."

—Paul Mason, economics editor for Channel 4 News, author of
Postcapitalism and *Live Working or Die Fighting:*
How the Working Class Went Global

"As these vivid case studies illustrate, the real sleeping dragon—China's enormous factory proletariat—is wide awake and fighting back on all fronts. Indeed, here is firsthand evidence that Chairman Xi Jinping may soon confront the largest labor rebellion in history."

—Mike Davis, professor emeritus, University of California, Riverside,
and author of *Planet of Slums*

"*China on Strike* is a much-needed, detailed account of labor struggle in the Pearl River Delta region, China's manufacturing industrial heartland. It is a story brilliantly told from migrant workers' own perspectives, about all that keeps this factory of the world moving."

—Hsiao-Hung Pai, author of *Scattered Sand:*
The Story of China's Rural Migrants

"This book breathes authenticity. *China on Strike* is a collection of oral histories created by a network of workers, students, students become workers, and intellectuals practicing in related fields, whose underlying concern is to make known what is really happening on the ground in China. The scenes they describe very much resemble the rank-and-file self-organization of workers in the United States in the early 1930s. Let us hope that as our Chinese comrades become more organized and powerful they are able to retain the wonderful vitality of the early actions described in this remarkable book."

—Staughton Lynd, labor historian and coeditor with Alice Lynd of
Rank and File: Personal H · · · ʃ

"*China on Strike* provides the most detailed and vivid accounts of migrant workers' struggles in the Pearl River Delta, the powerhouse of China's reform and industrialization. The struggles of these workers shed light on the future of the labor movement not only in China, but worldwide. A must-read book for readers concerned with labor activism and international solidarity!"

–Pun Ngai, Hong Kong Polytechnic University,
author of *Made in China* and *Migrant Labor in China*

"This book provides an exhaustive and vivid account of migrant workers' strikes in China. Many authors of this book are young, well-educated, and passionate labor activists. Through the eyes and hearts of these organic intellectuals, readers can feel how a new working class is creating itself in struggles. It will inspire imagination about the future of China, globalization, and the labor movement."

—Chris King-Chi Chan, City University of Hong Kong

"China is not only the elephant in the room of global capitalism but the site of one of the world's greatest ongoing labor upheavals. China's working class in formation has mounted mass strikes against all odds—a one-party dictatorship, 'unions' controlled by the Communist Party, waves of internal migration, and, of course, global capital itself. Yet, China's mostly young workers rebel in growing numbers, forcing concessions from the bureaucratic state as well as from giant corporations. *China on Strike* provides a unique view of the developing consciousness and actions of these daring workers as the strike movement of recent years took shape. This is a book that should be read by all those who care about the future possibilities of working-class power everywhere."

–Kim Moody, author of *In Solidarity: Essays on Working-Class Organization and Strategy in the United States*

"China has become not only the 'workshop' of the capitalist world but also the epicenter of the global class struggle. The workers in China are making history. This is the time to read *China on Strike*, a book about ordinary workers and worker-activists and how they fight for a better world tomorrow."

—Minqi Li, associate professor of economics, University of Utah

"Workers throughout the world are fighting wage cuts, bad working conditions, and runaway shops. Without rights or protections taken for granted elsewhere, Chinese workers have struck thousands of times over these and other issues. *China on Strike* gives voice to factory struggles rarely reported in the United States and confirms the central role played by a new generation of rank-and-file leaders. Their inspiring exercise of shop-floor power is worthy of close study by labor activists here."

—Steve Early, former CWA organizer and author of
Save Our Unions: Dispatches from a Movement in Distress

"Over the past two decades China has emerged as an industrial powerhouse, and the country's explosive growth has been a defining feature of the global economy. Now China's workers are taking center stage. *China on Strike* paints a vivid, firsthand picture of working conditions in the heart of China's 'manufacturing miracle,' the impetus for tens of thousands of job actions and labor disputes each year. The stories featured in *China on Strike* put to rest the notion that today's factory workers are helpless victims. On the contrary, they demonstrate that it's still possible to fight back at work and win, even against the world's most powerful corporations and an unbending, one-party state. The book is testament to the enduring power of solidarity, and the creativity that bubbles up when workers stand up and fight back."

—Mark Brenner, *Labor Notes*

China on Strike

Narratives of Workers' Resistance

Edited by Hao Ren

English edition edited by Zhongjin Li
and Eli Friedman

Haymarket Books
Chicago, Illinois

Published by
Haymarket Books
P.O. Box 180165
Chicago, IL 60618
773-583-7884
info@haymarketbooks.org
www.haymarketbooks.org

ISBN: 978-1-60846-522-4

Trade distribution:
In the US through Consortium Book Sales and Distribution,
www.cbsd.com
In the UK, Turnaround Publisher Services, www.turnaround-uk.com
In Canada, Publishers Group Canada, www.pgcbooks.ca
All other countries, Publishers Group Worldwide, www.pgw.com

This book was published with the generous support
of the Wallace Action Fund and Lannan Foundation.

Printed in Canada by union labor.

Cover art by Bec Young. Cover design by Rachel Cohen.

Library of Congress CIP Data is available.

1 3 5 7 9 10 8 6 4 2

Contents

Preface to the English Edition

Given China's current system, it is better to cut off the boss's
production.
—electronics worker in Shenzhen

China on Strike: Narratives of Workers' Resistance is the outcome of an
incredible collective effort by many people scattered across many countries. Not only is this book the most detailed account of the process
and outcomes of worker resistance in China available in English, it
is also an example of first-rate public sociology. It is hardly debatable
that China represents the future of global capitalism, but the stories
collected in this volume suggest that it is also the future of the labor
movement. In light of this, we have put together this English translation in the hopes of gaining greater international exposure for worker
struggles in China.

The book does not detail the entirety of worker struggles in China,
but rather is concerned with migrant workers in Guangdong Prov
ince's Pearl River Delta. "Migrant" in the Chinese context refers to the
270 million people who have left the countryside to work in the city.
Because of the restrictive household registration system (the *hukou*)
they are second-class citizens in urban areas, excluded from a variety
of social services. Migrants now constitute the large majority of the
workforce in many industries—including manufacturing, construction,
and low-end service jobs—but they by no means represent the entirety
of the working class.

Similarly, the Pearl River Delta is only one region in a vast country (see maps below). This area has attracted more manufacturers than anywhere else in China, and has been the most dynamic regional economy over the past thirty years. It has also attracted the most migrant workers and served as ground zero for expanding worker resistance. While it would be wrong to assume that Guangdong represents the future of China, worker struggles there are certainly more frequent and more intense than elsewhere. It is for these reasons that the editors have focused their activism and scholarship on this region.

Map 1: People's Republic of China

It is important for the reader to appreciate the process by which this book came to fruition. Although the book is the outcome of a collaborative effort, Hao Ren, the original Chinese edition editor, was largely responsible for shepherding it through to publication. After graduating from college, Hao Ren began working at an NGO in Guangdong Province in 2009, eventually leaving to take up work in a factory. She made contact with a number of Marxist-oriented university students who had also gone to work in factories, some for idealistic reasons, others simply because they needed the wages. This informally constituted network of activists began conducting interviews with workers in their spare time, with the specific aim of trying to establish a more systematic understanding of the causes, processes, and outcomes of strikes. In carefully considering the role of various types of actors—workers, managers, the union, NGOs, lawyers, and the state—these activists were also interested in compiling relevant practical knowledge that was then disseminated in industrial zones as a series of magazines. Without this network of people embedded in factories, it would have never been possible to get such detailed information. Strikes are still considered quite politically sensitive in China, and so it is almost always necessary to establish a high level of trust before people will openly discuss their experiences.

Map 2: The Pearl River Delta

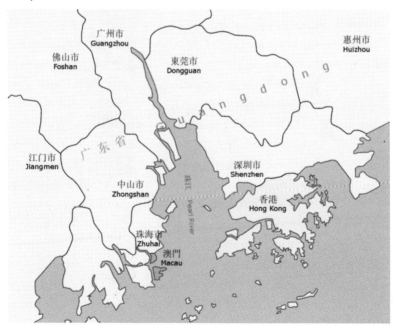

In 2009, through the International Center for Joint Labor Research at Sun Yat-sen University in Guangzhou, a group of students volunteered for a "Labor Materials Translation Group." Through steadily changing membership, this group has translated books, academic and popular articles, workers' blogs, films, legislation and ordinances, transcripts of meetings and lectures, education materials, and more from English to Chinese, and Chinese to English. The translation of this book was a collective, volunteer effort by numerous people on several continents who were associated with this translation group. Ellen David Friedman, a lecturer at Sun Yat-sen University, initiated the translation effort and helped recruit translators. Zhongjin Li was primarily responsible for overseeing the translation, and Kevin Lin, "ZSL," Sean Li, Thomas Peng, and Ralf Ruckus also made major contributions. There are instances in the original manuscript with obvious inconsistencies or unclarified information. In those cases, we added notes but aimed to stick as close as possible to the original text.

This volume is a shining example of public sociology. Certainly the stories we have included are based on careful research and observation by university students in China, but from the very outset, the participants in this project were primarily concerned with practical rather than just academic consequences. The researchers were embedded in the communities and workplaces that they were studying, often times working shoulder to shoulder with their *gongyou* (worker friends). Having been inspired by radical theory in the classroom, they sought to see for themselves what life was like in the workshop of the world. In other words, the researchers hoped to not only study but also inspire worker struggles. The accounts in this volume therefore serve as a sort of instruction manual for other workers considering direct action as a means to counter capital's rule. Workers who read these materials can learn about how to formulate demands and select representatives, the various strategies bosses use to coopt representatives, what to look for as signs that the boss might flee with unpaid debts, and even how to distinguish different categories of police. Thus, not only did this research bring students into the factory to produce new sociological knowledge, the outcomes of this research are of immediate practical value.

We, however, would like to suggest that the practical relevance is not limited to Chinese workers, but rather could serve as inspiration to activists globally. This begins by correcting a misperception about labor politics in China. Chinese workers are frequently depicted in the media and even in academic studies as complete victims, unable to conjure any resistance to the overbearing power of transnational capital and a deeply authoritarian Communist Party. In the West, we are told that it is our responsibility to act beneficently toward these pitiable souls by consuming ethically. Collective action and labor movements are simply not possible in a globalized world, so we should settle for individualized and marketized forms of sympathy.

Without diminishing the scale of labor rights violations in China or elsewhere in the global South, the stories in this volume suggest three things. First, labor resistance in China has grown as explosively as the country's GDP. Try as it might, capital cannot expand without constantly reproducing its historical antagonist, the working class. Second, despite the overwhelmingly long odds, direct confrontation at the point of production is more effective than nearly any other channel available to Chinese workers. Even if the power asymmetry between state and capital on the one side and workers on the other remains terrifying, victories—partial though they may be—are possible. And the evidence is clear that the effects of worker activism in China (including substantive collective bargaining and democratic elections following strikes, and new laws meant to address the root causes of strikes) have far exceeded the marginal improvements that have come about as a result of ethical consumerism. Finally, collective action is politically and socially the only sound basis for the development of a labor movement in China. One worker compared striking to the example set by Foxconn workers in 2010: "He emphasized the indispensability of collective discussions for any action that would help participants feel confident and empowered—rather than pessimistically committing suicide."

But the value of this book should not be limited to insights about how we should perceive the Chinese working class. Rather, we hope that the struggles of Chinese workers can help inspire similar forms of resistance elsewhere. Indeed, nominally "socialist" China presents in hyperbolic form many of the problems that those of us in the capitalist world experience: low wages, no benefits, lawlessness in the workplace, anti-union employers and governments, a broken system of political representation. As workers in mature capitalist countries see that they exert decreasing power through their unions or governments, while confronting ever more ruthless employers, what options are left? In more and more places around the world, it seems as if direct confrontation in the workplace and the community is the only option.

We do not want to seem Pollyannaish or to romanticize "unmediated antagonism." Indeed, partial victories or utter defeats are a common outcome for striking workers in China. Capital's geographic mobility remains a huge strategic advantage over labor, and this is something that a strike in a single workplace cannot overcome. Chinese workers remain unable to form durable organizations and are therefore prevented from acting politically at the class level. Even if workers have sometimes been successful in particular strikes, Chinese migrant workers still face a rigidly unequal citizenship regime, great precarity in all spheres of life, and an exclusionary and repressive political system. But if political power will be necessary to successfully counter these trends, as it certainly will be, then worker mobilization must serve as the foundation. There is every reason to believe that this will be as true outside of China as it is inside.

Zhongjin Li and Eli Friedman
December 2015

Preface

With the resurgence of capitalism in recent decades, labor movements in China have been increasingly active. So far, in addition to the struggle of workers in state-owned enterprises against restructuring reforms, protests organized by workers from the private factories in China's coastal regions have also dramatically increased in terms of scale, frequency, and duration.

The intensification of industrial actions undoubtedly has threatened the power of capital, and thus protests, especially in the form of strikes, have attracted much public attention within China. Since the level of official censorship varies at times, the media, NGOs, and academia have all become involved in reporting, studying, and even assisting the strikes. However, most studies merely express sympathy for workers, or propose suggestions to the state for sustaining "harmony" within the capital-labor relation. There has also been some degree of opportunism, with intellectuals attempting to inflate personal reputations. As a result, the discourse on this issue has been dominated by people with almost no real connection to workers, one result of which is that workers' own voices are often drowned out. Not surprisingly, we rarely read reports about labor struggles from workers' perspectives, not to mention records of the strike organizing process, documents, or analyses of lessons from the strikes.

The editor of this book, therefore, recorded a few narratives of these protests through face-to-face interviews conducted in 2010–12. These accounts focus on the causes, processes, consequences, and impact of these strikes, mainly in workers' own words. Most of the interviews are edited only for clarity.

This book is composed of three parts. Part I documents cases of workers' struggle against lockouts and factory closures, part II focuses on the struggle against wage reductions, and part III is devoted to the struggle for higher wages. It may seem to readers that this structure is "unbalanced" in that there are only two and three chapters, respectively, in parts I and III while part II includes ten. Nevertheless, the unbalanced structure corresponds to what we have witnessed: among various strikes taking place almost every day during the last twenty years, the most prevalent reason for collective protest is wage reduction.

We did not originally plan to compile these interviews for publication. Moreover, due to certain constraints, we were not able to scientifically "select" our interviewees. Readers may find many limitations in the book; for example, some representative cases were not included, and the structure of the book is still, more or less, rough. However, we hope this collection can intrigue or inspire readers in general and worker readers in particular. We also hope that more people will participate in the project, by speaking out or writing about worker protests they experienced or observed, or contributing to gathering more interviews in their own ways.

The work would not have been possible without the support of our friends who helped us make contact with workers, take notes during interviews, and edit a large amount of materials. We would like to thank them all. Working in factories to make a living, we often had limited time and resources to conduct our surveys; the work to continue the endeavor of recording and sharing workers' narratives at present and in the future is in dire need of volunteers who can help us find sources, transcribe recordings, participate in interviews, and help write the stories of the workers.

There will be more published oral histories of Chinese workers. Any kind of support or cooperation would be appreciated. For more information, please contact ghqting@gmail.com.

Hao Ren
September 4, 2011

Introduction

The Survival and Collective Struggles of Workers in China's Coastal Private Enterprises since the 1990s

Qin Ling
July 1, 2011

The restoration of capitalism in China didn't happen overnight. Market reform began in rural areas and gradually proceeded with the "household responsibility system."[1] Most rural families received their own plots by the early 1980s. Grain output increased due to a number of factors, including the increased enthusiasm of peasants,[2] the expansion of water conservancy construction, and the widespread use of chemical fertilizers, pesticides, and biological technologies. Peasants' earnings grew due to increases in the price of agricultural products. However, newly self-sufficient peasants didn't have a good life immediately. Though gains in income allowed them to meet their basic needs of food and clothing, peasants still needed other means to cover family expenses. At the beginning of the 1980s, the development of TVEs (township and village enterprises) provided new sources of income. But by the beginning of the 1990s, the development potential of agriculture had come to an end, and increasing taxes and dues imposed an increasingly severe burden on peasants. In the new market economy,

1. Editors' note: a system in which rural households became the primary unit of economic production rather than the communes that had existed previously.
2. Editors' note: for receiving their own plots of land.

1

the first generation of migrant workers emerged out of the great surplus of rural laborers flowing into the cities.

In 1979, the central government decided to create SEZs (special economic zones) in places such as Shenzhen to attract entrepreneurial investment. Such places gradually became the preferred destinations for the first generation of migrant workers from rural areas. These were the real "peasant workers."[3] Some of them became workers on factory assembly lines, some on construction sites, and some in service industries. Most of them remained engaged in agriculture; working in cities was just a means for them to make extra money. So there was nothing they could not bear, including the high intensity of factory work, job insecurity, and low wages. They were not incorporated into the cities and had to return to the countryside when they were ready to marry. Female workers would stay home for a few years until their children went to school and then would go back to work to support their families. Some of them tried to start their own businesses with accumulated funds after working outside for a few years; some had to return home to work the fields after they were considered too old to be hired by factories. In general, there were deep ties between the first generation of migrant workers in coastal cities and their rural hometowns.

Documents about the struggles of coastal migrant workers before the 1990s, if they ever existed, are quite hard to find. Let's put this aside temporarily. This chapter focuses on the survival and struggles of migrant workers in the coastal cities after 1990. The stated facts are based primarily on my experiences and observations of labor NGOs and secondarily on a series of interviews with industrial workers in the Pearl River Delta. The formation of the working class in private enterprises of the coastal cities, and their survival and struggles, are highly correlated to the economic situation of different periods, industrial development, and government policies. This introduction summarizes four stages.

---

3. Editors' note: "Peasant workers" (*nongmingong*) is a Chinese phrase that refers to people who maintain rural residency (or hukou) while working outside of their place of residency, and primarily in large urban areas.

wage increases and improvements in living conditions. Some asked for significant salary increases; in three companies strikers demanded a 50 percent increase.

It was said that Canon's workers already enjoyed the highest salary and best welfare benefits of all the foreign-funded enterprises in Zhuhai City. Taking monthly salary as an example, the lowest level for its workers was 620 yuan, with the management staff at 884 yuan, and the highest at 1,300 yuan. So why did such a large-scale strike take place in such a "good" factory?

According to investigations at the time, there were several possible reasons:

1. The inflation rate was much higher than the salary increases. The Consumer Price Index (CPI) of Zhuhai City in the first quarter of 1993 was as high as 22 percent, and workers were quite dissatisfied because pay raises were generally less than 10 percent.
2. The work environment was bad and mandatory overtime was excessive. Private companies like the Qianshan Shoe Factory of Yue Yuen Industrial Holdings often required its workers to work overtime. There were four hours of overtime every day in the first half of May. Workers had to work from 7 a.m. to 1 or 2 a.m. in the morning, exhausted, and without any food in the evening. This treatment triggered 460 workers to strike. Some companies' workshops did not have ventilation systems, resulting in noxious gases that jeopardized the workers' health.
3. The living conditions of workers in some foreign-funded companies were miserable. Despite the requirements of the Zhuhai municipal government that enterprises provide workers with proper living facilities before starting operation, a lot of foreign-funded companies did not provide housing for their staff and workers. Facing high rents outside, workers had to cram together in poor living quarters. A damp and filthy room might house more than ten people, crowded together like sardines with two people sharing a single bed. Each tenant might have to pay 50 to 100 yuan as rent, while the housing allowances

from the company might only be 20 to 30 yuan. Some workers complained about the bad food offered in the company's canteen and the difficulty in accessing water.

The result was that the government intervened to mediate these conflicts,[10] and demanded the following: that all workers resume work and negotiate later; that the factories change their improper practices, and that workers abandon their "unreasonable" wage demands (i.e. those that were higher than the local minimum wage); that companies adjust or increase subsidies for housing, food, and transportation. These interventions rapidly ended the strike movement in these foreign-funded companies.

The cases mentioned above were comparatively successful, positive struggles. However, spontaneous revolts out of desperation were actually more common.

2. 2003–2007

2.1 Background

China's economy grew rapidly with its entry into the World Trade Organization (WTO) and integration into global capitalism. Foreign investment poured into China seeking cheap labor. The hukou (household registration) system[11] created an impediment to economic development. The Regulation of Custody and Repatriation, which had restricted the free flow of labor, was abolished after the Sun Zhigang case in 2003.[12] From then on, rural migrant workers have had somewhat more stability in the city, and higher expectations of working and

10. Editors' note: The government serves as the regulator and arbitrator for all enterprises, especially when the employer and employee cannot reach an agreement on their own.
11. The hukou system links provision of social service to place, which practically speaking means that many migrant workers are excluded from such services when they are in the city.
12. Editors' note: Sun Zhigang was a migrant in Guangdong who was beaten to death in custody after being detained for not having his ID card with him.

living in the cities. At the same time, starting in 2004, there developed a "shortage of migrant workers" (which means that the supply of low-wage job positions was increasing relative to demand), allowing workers to have more job opportunities and to take action if their rights and interests had been violated.

The basic situation of workers improved somewhat as more resistance emerged. Compared with the 1990s, labor intensity in some industries was reduced to a certain extent, especially in large-scale electronics factories. Generally speaking, workers had fewer than three hours of overtime per day, still far more than the thirty-six hour monthly maximum overtime stipulated in the Labor Law.[13] The prevalence of industrial injuries and occupational diseases was somewhat reduced. The scolding and beating of workers by management, which was common in the 1990s, also greatly declined.

From 2001 to 2007, the Chinese economy grew rapidly as measured by double-digit growth in GDP (Table 1). However, in the same period, workers' income increased very slowly (Table 2). Taking Shenzhen for example, the minimum wage inside the SEZ increased by only 36 yuan from 2001 to 2004. Outside the SEZ wages increased only 40 yuan during the same period, while the average growth rate of China's GDP was roughly 9.4 percent. The workers who were creating the economic miracle had to ceaselessly work overtime just to sustain their basic livelihood. If there is some space for them to struggle, they will create another kind of miracle.

---

13. According to Article 41 in the Labor Law, "The employing unit may extend working hours due to the requirements of its production or business after consultation with the trade union and laborers, but the extended working hours for a day shall generally not exceed one hour; if such extension is called for due to special reasons, the extended hours shall not exceed three hours a day under the condition that the health of laborers is guaranteed. However, the total extension in a month shall not exceed thirty-six hours."

Table 1. Annual GDP growth rate in China, 2001 to 2008[14]

Year	Growth Rate of GDP
2001	8.3%
2002	9.1%
2003	10.0%
2004	10.1%
2005	10.4%
2006	11.6%
2007	13.0%
2008	8.9%

Table 2. Minimum wage standards in Shenzhen City, 2001 to 2008[15]

Year	Monthly Wage in yuan	
	Inside the SEZ	Outside the SEZ
2001	574	440
2002	595	460
2003	600	460
2004	610	480
2005	690	580
2006	810	700
2007	850	750
2008	1000	900

Under the pressure of continuing worker resistance, as well as the good economic situation, the government was forced to set higher wage standards. This attempt to pacify workers gave rise to a seemingly huge increase of wages from 2005 to 2008. But these figures do not necessarily indicate that the material condition of workers greatly improved. Anyone with work experience in coastal areas could easily tell us that the prices

14. Editors' note: These tables are not cited in the original. World Bank data show somewhat higher growth rates, but the general pattern of increasing growth through 2007 is the same.
15. Shenzhen Minimum Wage Standards Act, various years.

of commodities went up even faster than wages. Immediately before the minimum wage standard was raised every year, the cost of housing, food, and various articles had already gone up, usually more significantly than the minimum wage standard. Many medium and small-sized factories even paid workers less than the local minimum wage. Workers' struggles did not come to an end with the raising of the nominal wage, but led to another round of resistance.

During this period, workers' pent-up anger came out in torrents. There was a concentrated surge of strikes from 2004 to 2006, clustered in large foreign-funded electronic factories with relatively good wages and welfare benefits. The reasons were: 1) Such factories were more profitable; compared to those small-scale and low-profit industries, they had more capacity to give wage increases and improvements in living conditions for workers; 2) Workers in such factories were more confident in fighting for improvements because they had inside information about the profitability of these factories; 3) Workers had a strong sense of the unfairness of the situation; their relatively good wage was almost nothing compared with the huge profits earned by the factory owners.

The main features of strikes during this period were that they were female-worker dominated, were unorganized and spontaneous, and that they used methods such as roadblocks, demonstrations, blocking government offices, and collective petitions. Such strikes often took place in large-scale enterprises. Roadblocks and demonstrations were seen in a strike involving 16,000 workers in the Japanese Uniden Electronics factory in 2004.[16] Three thousand workers in Shenzhen's Haiyan factory went on strike and blocked the road in October 2004. Five thousand workers from Changying factory went on strike because of labor disputes and stormed the Nantou checkpoint[17] in April 2004.[18]

---

16. Wu Ji, "The Whole Story of the Worker Struggle in Uniden Electronics Factory," June 3, 2011, http://www.laborpoetry.com/forum.php?mod=viewthread&tid=310.
17. Editors' note: This checkpoint separates the SEZ from the rest of Shenzhen. In the early days of reform, there was not free movement between these two areas, so the checkpoint functioned as a semi-border.
18. "Xixiang Street Labor Administration Office Coordinates Labor Relation According to Law, Addresses Both the Symptoms and Root Causes, and Constructs

Almost at the same time, strikes took place in four shoe factories of the Taiwanese Xing'ang Group in Dongguan City, including Weichuangli Company, Feihuang Company, Aimeili Company, Baoxin Company, and Emerson Company.[19] Workers in different factories kept encouraging and supporting each other through coordinated actions. Unfortunately, most information about the strikes was censored. However, the consciousness and actions of workers were quietly changing.

With limited experience and few precedents, workers' acts of resistance were very spontaneous and fierce. The government was quite tough when dealing with workers' collective struggles, and—due to lack of experience with such abrupt, fierce, and large-scale strikes—resorted to direct repression. All strikes of a certain scale would confront large police forces. The forces included armed police, public security guards, antiriot troops, security scouts, militiamen, and even traffic wardens. They served not only to frighten the workers psychologically but also physically. In the cases of roadblocks and demonstrations, workers were often beaten by policemen. Sometimes the leaders or other activist workers were even arrested.

2.2 Key Features of Strikes in This Period[20]

Causes of the Strikes

From 2003 to 2008, many strikes broke out. Some were triggered by workers' dissatisfaction with wages or because overtime pay was lower than the local minimum wage. Some were caused by workers' demands for economic compensation, including repayment of unpaid wages due to bankruptcy, factory relocation, or runaway bosses. And others were

---

Harmonious Labor-Management Relation," from Shenzhen Municipal People's Congress website.

19. Editors' note: The inconsistency in the number of factories experiencing strikes appears in the original text.

20. Editors' note: We have deleted an approximately 1,500-word section from the original that provides an overview of the strike discussed in part III, "Strike in a Large Electronics (Motor) Factory in 2007." While this has resulted in a minor deviation from the original text, we found that all of the information from this deleted section is covered in part III, chapter 14.

caused by work scheduling problems or terrible food. Clearly, there were diverse causes of the strikes and some even started over minor incidents. For instance, a strike in a Taiwanese factory was initiated because a worker found an insect in her food. Yet these seemingly random events were the inevitable result of the factories' wage erosion offensive and the accumulated resentment of workers.

Workers' Representatives during the Strikes

Strike leaders were sometimes basic-level managers and technical workers, which improved the chance of winning since workers could be better organized. But leaders of this kind were more easily bribed by the bosses and willing to accept underhanded secret dealings. Some strikes were initiated secretly by workers who had worked in the factory for a long time and were generally regarded with respect. Factory management usually required that workers choose representatives to negotiate after a strike started. As there were many cases of retaliation against workers' representatives, the workers were uneasy about selecting representatives, which sometimes resulted in factories appointing representatives. Unsurprisingly, this often sidelined key strike organizers during negotiations. After selecting representatives, some other problems emerged: The representatives had difficulty clearly articulating demands. This phenomenon demonstrated the premature quality of these strikes—they were unorganized and unplanned. Additionally, workers lacked awareness of collective struggle. Even though some of them had experienced strikes before, their consciousness and actions were still undeveloped and they lacked confidence.

Actions of Different Groups during Strikes

Women workers were in the majority of such factories and occupied key positions in production. Older workers with heavier family burdens were comparatively less productive and didn't dare to lead out of fear of losing their jobs. Foremen and technicians seldom participated in strikes and their role was usually to persuade (actively or passively) workers to resume work. In the cases mentioned above, the foremen played a comparatively passive role. Except for the team leader (discussed in chapter 14) who was later promoted to supervisor, most foremen neither actively participated in the strike, nor forcefully demanded the resumption of work. When asked to deal with the restoration of production, they just went through the motions.

The Spread of Information during the Strikes

The use of mobile phones and the Internet facilitated communication among workers. In one case discussed in part III, information about the strikes was first spread through hometown networks. In influential strikes, photos and BBS[21] messages sent by workers were common. In some cases, handbills and leaflets were made by strike leaders to encourage other workers and to disseminate strike information. Unfortunately, these materials were often just "testimony" and for making "accusations." There was almost no conscious documentation of the strike process, not to mention summarizing the experiences and lessons learned.

Propagation of Strike Experiences

Cases of collective resistance with comparatively good results could serve as models for later strikes in nearby factories. Such examples gave other workers greater confidence and guidance. In 2003, one strike participant said in an interview, "Right before our strike, there had been strikes in two nearby factories, and the roadblock was the most common tactic." She also summarized her experiences as follows: Male workers were readily arrested if they offended the cops during a strike. But cops did not dare put their hands on female workers (if they did, there would be accusations of "sexual harassment" immediately from some women). Some other interviewees added, "It's more likely for the boss to meet our demands during the busy season when there are many orders waiting to be completed." Regrettably, such experiences were not shared as widely as possible with other workers. It is difficult to consolidate struggles isolated in one factory, at one time, into oppor-

---

21. Editors' note: This refers to "bulletin board system," a method of Internet-based communication that was popular in China at the time.

tunities for more united action. There is no credible evidence showing any deliberate cross-factory unified action.

The Unity and Mutual Aid of Workers among Strikes

If worker representatives were detained in a strike, other workers would usually voluntarily stand up to protect them, so long as they were respected as leaders. Additionally, female workers would voluntarily protect leaders and their male colleagues when management attempted to find out who the activists were, even in strikes whose participants were mainly female. Female workers protected the representatives from being arrested in the strike in Youli Electronics factory in December 2004—and this was not an exception. In many strikes, workers would donate funds to cover representatives' transportation, room and board, and legal fees when they were filing formal petitions. This indicates some measure of self-sacrifice and labor solidarity. When talking about the series of strikes motivated by the implementation of the 2008 Labor Contract Law, a worker mentioned that at that time workers from many factories who blocked the road were often arrested and detained. Worker representatives later went to the government with petitions of support and donations from other workers.

3. 2008–2009

3.1 State Policies, Laws and Regulations, and Workers' Resistance

Workers' spontaneous, undisciplined, "irrational" resistance before 2008 usually took a somewhat violent form—expressing workers' anger and attracting societal attention—so that their problems could be solved more quickly and properly. Commonly used methods included roadblocks and petitions, which greatly displeased the government and capitalists. These actions impacted both "production discipline" and "social order," and made it difficult for capitalists to maintain an environment conducive for exploiting workers. Thus, the government began to implement a series of laws, including the Labor Contract Law and the Labor Dispute Mediation and Arbitration Law. The government's purpose was to incorporate workers' resistance into the state apparatus, establish legal channels acceptable to the capitalist class, and avoid economic losses caused by disruption in production.

The implementation of the Labor Contract Law really caught the attention of capitalists, mainstream intellectuals, and the media. It provoked an uproar from the capitalists, who argued that the Labor Contract Law would cause an increase in labor cost. At the same time they prepared themselves for the impact of the law. For example, Huawei required its workers to resign and then compete for reemployment,[22] so they could avoid signing non-fixed-term labor contracts[23] with existing workers. Walmart callously fired workers.[24] Other factories established new labor contracts with their workers in order to void their seniority, which caused a wave of strikes. One interviewee mentioned that a series of strikes took place in Longgang, a town in Shenzhen, where the interviewee worked: "At the end of 2007, strikes broke out almost every day. And the participants came from all kinds of industries and jobs. They did not go to work, gathering around the gate or wandering in the square. The strikes were all in large factories with at least two hundred or three hundred workers. Such factories as Yunchang, Dahua, and Jingchang employed thousands of workers. At that time, the new Labor Contract Law had just been implemented. Workers lost their seniority after the bosses terminated their existing labor contracts, so workers went on strike."

22. "Huawei Encourages Its Employees to Resign by Paying One-Billion-Yuan Compensation in Order to Circumvent Labor Contract Law," *Zhongguo Wang* (China.com.cn), November 2, 2007, http://www.china.com.cn/law/txt/2007 -11/02/content_9162383.htm.
23. Editors' note: "Non-fixed-term contracts" refer to contracts without an expiration date. Removing non-fixed-term employees is much easier and less expensive for employers.
24. "Walmart in China Fires 110 Employees Due to the Shock Wave of Labor Contract Law," *Dayang Wang* (Dayoo.com), November 5, 2007, http://news.dayoo .com/finance/news/2007-11/05/content_3128725.htm.

The implementation of the Labor Contract Law prompted China's capitalist class to publicly assert their interests. When the government subsequently called for public comments on a draft of the Guangdong Province Regulations on the Democratic Management of Enterprises, both Hong Kong capitalists with mainland investments and the Japanese Chamber of Commerce and Industry in China openly opposed the regulations. Though Chinese domestic capitalists argued for their own interests under the disguise of the ambiguous term "other stakeholders,"[25] it showed that they were upholding their class interests in an increasingly conscious and organized manner. Meanwhile, workers were protecting their interests defensively and in a less organized manner—because workers did not have their own organizations or media through which they could openly express their class interests.

Besides channeling workers' movements through the new laws, the government was also attempting to limit workers' "destructive" actions. For instance, actions such as roadblocks and collective petitions were pronounced to be illegal. At the end of 2009, the Shenzhen municipal government issued a "Notice on Dealing with Abnormal Petition Behaviors in Accordance with the Law,"[26] which defined fourteen behaviors as "abnormal petition behaviors." At the same time, workers who went on strike by blocking roads were arrested, with the "leading troublemakers" detained. As a result, workers' collective resistance gradually grew more self-contained, seeking to be in accordance with the law as much as possible. This was indicated by a decreasing frequency of roadblocks, sit-downs, and demonstrations. More resistance took the form of strikes within factories or industrial sabotage.

---

25. Deng Yuwen, "Ideas Were Solicited for Guangdong Enterprise Democratic Management Regulation; Is It Almost Impossible to Allow One Third Employees to Propose Wage Negotiation?" *Nanfang Ribao* (South Daily), August 27, 2010. In the article, it was pointed out that *other stakeholders* (editor's emphasis) also raised many ideas and suggestions, mainly represented by "Six Concerns," according to which they demanded revisions of the new law.

26. "Notice on Dealing with Abnormal Petition Behaviors in Accordance with the Law" was co-issued by Shenzhen Municipal Court, the People's Procuratorate, the Justice Bureau, and the Police Department in November 2009.

3.2 The Economic Crisis and Workers' Resistance

The global economic crisis, beginning in the second half of 2008, impacted China gradually yet deeply. As street protests erupted in major capitalist countries in the West, workers in China voted with their feet—they were forced to return home due to job loss. When profitability deteriorated and overtime was cut, some workers left their factories because of reduced wages, while some factories took the initiative of cutting jobs. According to my investigation in a Shenzhen industrial park in 2009, many factories laid off 50 percent or more of their workforce. At the same time, factories raised their hiring requirements—they demanded better education, higher skills, more experience, and even better personal appearance.[27]

During the crisis, bosses were expecting the arrival of a "cold winter" for their enterprises, and thus asked the government to postpone the implementation of related laws and to provide them with preferential policies. For example, Lee Yuen Fat, chairman of the Hong Kong Diecasting and Foundry Association, wrote an open letter about the government's policies during the financial crisis, demanding that government help both capital and labor through the "cold winter."[28] His policy suggestions included raising the export tax rebate to its 2005 level, freezing the minimum wage in the coming year, and postponing the implementation of the new Labor Contract Law. Although the domestic capitalist class had not openly voiced its needs in an organized way, the pro-capitalist state—having shared interests with capital—was well aware of the necessity of "easing their burden." According to a talk by Jiang Ling, vice mayor of the city of Dongguan, on November 6, the Dongguan government suggested the Central and Guangdong governments should reduce the pressure of the Labor Contract Law and slow the increase of the minimum wage, in order to aid medium- and small-

27. See Shen Mei, "The Plight of Pearl River Delta Region Workers and Labor Conflicts: Trends since the Onset of the Financial Crisis," *China Left Review*, September 14, 2010, http://chinaleftreview.org/?p=488 for details of workers' living conditions under the impact of the crisis of 2008 and 2009.

28. "Hong Kong Diecasting & Foundry Association: Suspend the Implementation of New Labor Contract Law in Response to the Economic Crisis," November 10, 2008, http://business.sohu.com/20081110/n260550390.shtml.

scale enterprises through the "cold winter."[29] Meanwhile, the Ministry of Human Resources and Social Security promised to postpone raising the minimum wage standard for all enterprises. In 2009, minimum wage standards were kept constant throughout China.[30]

Worker resistance during this period was mainly provoked by factory closures, bankruptcies or relocations, or runaway bosses. Because governments in many places partially covered workers' unpaid wages, the social impact of workers' collective action was significantly reduced. For example, according to the Regulations on Back Pay Protection in Shenzhen Special Economic Zone (issued in Shenzhen in 1996, implemented in 1997, and further amended in 2008), the government collects "back pay protection deposits" from enterprises so that when the enterprises go bankrupt and the bosses flee, the government can cover workers' back pay. Thus workers' resistance of this type usually ended when they received their back pay.

In response to the crisis, the central government poured trillions of yuan into the economy in 2008 to stimulate investment and domestic demand. Local governments also attempted to finance large-scale infrastructure construction. All this investment created jobs for workers who had already returned home. Owing to these factors, workers' collective resistance declined to some degree.

3.3 Characteristics of Workers' Collective Struggle at This Stage[31]

Struggles during the economic crisis displayed the following characteristics:

1. Strikes were primarily defensive fights over economic needs. During the economic crisis, bosses were organized to collectively discuss ways to deal with the crisis. Their hope was to transfer the

---

29. "Dongguan's Deputy Mayor Suggests to Slowdown the Implementation of Labor Contract Law," *Jinan Ribao* (Jinan Daily), September 26, 2008.
30. Editors' note: In China, municipal governments set minimum wage standards.
31. Editors' note: As above, we have decided to delete a short section (more than 900 words) describing a strike. It repeats in condensed form the material from "Interview with a worker on Strike in a Shenzhen Factory" in part II.

cost of the crisis to the workers as much as possible. Workers were on the defensive. Thus, they would not take action unless they were confronted with various pressures from work and wage reductions.

2. Workers' demands were mainly focused on punitive policies that led to wage reductions, such as punishments and excessive mandatory days off. They demanded that factories pay back wages and overtime compensation. In bankrupt factories where bosses had run away, the main strike tactic was for workers to block roads or the gates of factories in order to pressure the local government to pay compensation.

3. Bosses were more organized, united, and aware of their class interests. During this time, their degree of organization improved significantly. Furthermore, their attitude toward workers was hypocritical. During strikes, the boss often acted kindly to the workers, and would blame the management who directly caused conflicts (for example, whichever manager had designed the wage system) while promising to meet workers' demands. This kind of insincerity could cause workers to let down their guard, thus masking the fundamental antagonism between labor and capital.

4. With the development of the Internet and cell phones, workers have more ways to publicize their demands. Nonetheless, at this stage, workers relied more on media reports, partially because workers believe in the "fairness" and "impartiality" of the media, and partially because of the fact that strikes reported in the media were more likely to achieve positive results for workers. To my knowledge, workers tried to make contact with the media in the majority of strikes.

4. 2010 to the Present

According to a survey conducted by the National Bureau of Statistics, industrial production started to recover in 2009 and profitability increased after a big decline.[32] In early 2010, the mainstream media

---

32. Director of National Statistics Bureau, Ma Jiantang, "National Economy

in coastal cities sensationalized the "labor shortage" issue. On top of that, jobs had been created after the central government implemented a four-trillion-yuan (around $585 billion) stimulus package mainly devoted to infrastructure projects. Workers generally had higher expectations for remuneration. Nevertheless, the improved remuneration did not arrive as expected, which triggered a rising tide of strikes nationwide. Among them, heavy attention was devoted to the Nanhai Honda strike from May 17 to June 1 in 2010, as well as subsequent strikes for higher wages in the automobile industry.

An investigation released by the All China Federation of Unions branch in Huadu District of Guangzhou showed that the auto production district experienced a series of strikes for higher wages in late February to mid-March: Workers at Yorozu Bao Mit Auto went on strike on February 27; workers at Alpha Corporation, Hexi Machinery, and Xichuan and Tacle automotive seat factories learned from the strikes at Yorozu Bao Mit and organized their own strikes on March 11; the next day, workers at Mahle, Rhythm, and GSK-NANJO Auto Parts went on strike one after another. The report also revealed the root cause of these strikes: "Wages had been stagnant for almost eight years despite the rising profitability and expansion of the plants. Considering the recent soaring living expenses for urban residents, many workers suffered from a decline in their real wages." In addition, excessive mandatory overtime and underpayment of wages in violation of labor law were also important causes of the strikes.[33]

Increased strike activity was not restricted to the Pearl River Delta but also appeared in other industrial parks all over China. "From 2005 to 2009, workers in the Dalian Development Zone had average annual wage increases of 5.7%, or about 45 yuan per year." From late May to late August, around seventy thousand workers from more than seven-

Achieved a Recovery and Rebound in 2009," National Bureau of Statistics of the People's Republic of China, January 21, 2010, http://www.stats.gov.cn/tjsj/zxfb/201001/t20100121_12629.html.
33. Huang Guifu and Wang Zhiguang, "Survey and Thoughts Regarding Labor-Management Conflicts in Several Enterprises in Huadu District of Guangzhou," *Zhongguo Gongyun* (Chinese Workers' Movement), no. 5 (2010).

ty factories in Dalian Development Area went on strike. As a result, workers received an average wage hike of 300 yuan per person.[34]

In January 2010, two thousand workers in United Win Technology Limited in Suzhou (Yangtze River Delta) launched a strike in response to a rumored cancellation of the year-end bonus. The underlying cause was an extremely low wage and high intensity of work over a long period of time, as well as bonuses and benefits frequently being withheld. Another important cause underlying this strike was the hexyl hydride (also called n-hexane) poisoning in 2009. In February, around a thousand workers in the Lacquer Craft factory in Dongguan went on strike. One month later, workers at the Dabang Footwear factory in Dongguan tried the same thing, as did the workers at the Canon factory in Shenzhen. In fact, the number of workers and factories involved in the rising tide of strikes during the first half of 2010 was so large as to make it difficult, if not impossible, to catalogue them all.

The strikes in this period shared a few key characteristics:

1. Workers were on the offensive. Compared to the previous strikes, which mainly sought to defend against wage arrears and reductions, the strikes in this period raised offensive demands, primarily related to wage increases.

2. Workers were united and dedicated during the tortuous and difficult process of the half-month strike at Honda. It was a great step forward for workers to demand restructuring[35] of the trade union. The success in achieving wage increases encouraged and directly inspired other strikes in the same industry nationwide, such as the ones at Foshan Fengfu Auto Parts, Foshan Transmission, Siu Lam Honda, Wuhan Auto Parts, Nansha Denso, Tianjin Toyota, Alei Siti Auto Parts, NHK-UNI Spring, Atsumitec,

---

34. "The Strike Wave in Dalian Involved 70,000 Participants from 73 Enterprises and ended in a Wage Increase by 34.5%," *Fenghuang Wang* (ifeng.com), September 19, 2010, http://finance.ifeng.com/news/special/cxcmzk/20100919/2636845.shtml.
35. Editors' note: "Restructuring" implies holding new elections for firm-level union representatives. But this takes place within the official union structure—it does *not* imply formation of an independent union.

and Omron. The high profitability of the automobile industry allowed management to make concessions, albeit limited ones. As a result, strikes resulted in wage increases in all cases.

3. The official union generally took a tough stance toward workers, especially in the notorious incident of beating workers during the Honda strike. On May 22, company management fired the strike representatives, which infuriated workers and the strike soon extended to the entire plant. On May 31 when workers learned that the "union stewards" shamelessly beat their co-workers, they got so angry that most of them who had already returned to work immediately left the plant again. Some local unions took lessons from these responses and changed their attitudes. In the later Nansha Denso strike, the local union—the self-proclaimed "representative of workers"—paid lip service to opposing police intervention against the strikers and offered to negotiate. The strike ended six days later. From another point of view, unions realized that in order to better control workers, they needed to establish authority among their constituents. Therefore they started making efforts to act "kindly."

4. The attitude of management was also tough. Again taking the Nansha Denso strike as an example, workers put forward their demands as early as during the spring festival (Chinese New Year), but they never received any response from management. As one cadre in the union branch in Nansha District said, "The local union had collected three demands from workers: 1) to increase wages by 100 yuan; 2) to install a heating system in the dorms; 3) to double the wage rate for overtime work at night. However, after the demands were submitted to management, there was no positive feedback except that they would provide a free dinner for the overtime workers at night." When the strike broke out on June 21, workers actually did not put forward their demands in advance. But the union cadre claimed, "the boss was so active that he declared that if workers returned to work immediately, no one would be blamed, air conditioners

would be installed right away, and wages would be raised by 450 yuan or so. Yet, he also demanded that workers decide and return to work within ten minutes; otherwise, he would implement tough measures, such as calling the police." But the boss's pressure didn't work. The union cadre was concerned that if the boss were too tough it would escalate the dispute, making the workers more determined to strike. Therefore they made efforts to mediate between management and the workers, and also attempted to figure out who the strike leaders were. Zeng Qinghong, vice president of Guangzhou Automobile Industry Group Corporation, also came to assist. Zeng had recently mediated the Honda strike. Perhaps because of their class position, bosses tended to act like "bad guys." Or maybe they thought that workers would give up as long as they intimidated them as usual. Or maybe bosses had a tacit agreement with the capitalist state about the division of labor: one plays "good cop" and the other "bad cop." Regardless, the militancy, persistence, and solidarity workers demonstrated in this strike went well beyond the expectations of their bosses.

5. During the process two new actors emerged: Zeng Qinghong and Chang Kai. Zeng was sitting on the board of directors of Honda and also had previously worked as an executive deputy general manager. As mentioned above, he was also the vice president of Guangzhou Automobile Industry Group Corporation.[36] As a result, he played a neutral and moderate role of authority during the strike wave. He utilized his dual positions as management as well as deputy to the People's Congress to gain trust from workers in order to mediate the industrial conflicts. Workers also had some expectations of him simply because, as some of them described, "He is the deputy to the People's Congress and the big boss, so he ought to keep his word."

36. Nanhai Honda is a completely Japanese-invested firm. But the assembly plant it supplies is a joint venture between Honda and the state-owned Guangzhou Automobile Industry Group Corporation.

During the negotiations, he persuaded workers to reduce their demands. He repeatedly told worker representatives that the average wage in the machinery processing industry in Foshan City was only 1,810 yuan. Therefore increasing their wages to 2,100 yuan already represented the highest level in the industry within the region, so workers should not demand more.[37]

Professor Chang Kai is a renowned expert on labor relations. He worked as a legal advisor for workers in the Honda strike. He strived to influence workers to accept the following two ideas: 1) The wage increase is not the top priority. "It is certainly good to have a wage increase. But raising wages some tens or even hundreds of yuan isn't the most important thing. The key is that management acknowledges workers' status and rights."[38] 2) Strikers should return to work during the bargaining process. "Chang Kai told the worker representatives that according to international conventions, workers absolutely should not strike when collective bargaining is in process. This kind of strike is not permitted by law."[39]

On the one hand, Professor Chang Kai expressed his sympathy and understanding for striking workers. As he said, "Either initiating a strike or participating in a strike should definitely not be a hasty move for workers, but rather should only be decided on after repeated consideration."[40] On the other hand, he suggested the government should play a neutral role between management and workers. "Government should behave equitably and neutrally as the third party, by carefully investigating and analyzing the cause of the strike, mediating between management and workers, as well as facilitating and presiding over the settlement of the

37. "The Whole Story of Collective Bargaining in Nanhai Honda," *Zhongguo Gongren* (Chinese Workers) no. 9, 2010.
38. Ibid.
39. Ibid.
40. Chang Kai, "How Should Government Deal with Worker Strikes," *Caijing*, August 5, 2010, http://www.caijing.com.cn/2010-08-05/110492061.html.

disputes between the two parties through collective bargaining."[41]

6. Along with the increase in struggles and accumulated experience, the working class has become more and more confident. In general, workers' education has significantly improved. Thanks to the widespread use of social media, worker struggles have adopted increasingly flexible forms. The strikes in the first half of 2010 witnessed a variety of attempts to use the Internet, including speaking via QQ chat software, exchanging information and ideas in online forums, and uploading all kinds of strike photos and live videos in order to give the strikes more public exposure. However, workers have not been aware that the media, government, and elite professionals are, by their very nature, assistants of the ruling class.

5. Conclusion

What sorts of treatment and practical resistance have various generations of workers experienced while creating enormous wealth? How can these workers be united to strive together for the liberation of the working class? This article has sketched the work experiences and struggles of Chinese workers over the last two decades. Due to space limitations, as well the constraints of my own experience and knowledge, I am not able to explore and document many issues. I would appreciate if you could help, for example, by conducting worker interviews, interviews with NGO staff, or even working in factories. Other contributions, such as assisting in transcribing interview recordings and organizing archival materials, would also be welcome. It is my hope that more and more allies would commit themselves to the task of worker revolution, with everyone contributing in their own way.

---

41. Ibid.

Part I: Struggles against Factory Closures

Under normal circumstances, workers are likely to suffer disproportionately during factory closures. They not only lose their jobs but also frequently are unable to claim back wages. These cases of strikes following closures show how workers resisted, how they got their wages back, and how a few even received additional compensation. Whether companies shut down because of bankruptcy, relocation, or bosses secretly running off, workers are frequently faced with wage arrears and deductions. In most cases, because the boss runs off, the factory is not operating, and workers cannot apply forms of struggle like slowdowns or strikes that they can when the factory is in operation. Therefore, the government becomes the target of their struggle. The authorities use all kinds of measures to pacify, deceive, or break the struggles of workers. Unless workers are prepared to give up their interests, they usually have to "step up" their actions: block roads, act collectively, and amplify their impact through media in order to push the government to act quickly. Even if that happens, usually workers get only as far as making the government pay the wages and wage arrears the boss embezzled before the factory closed. In many places, even that part of the wages is not paid in full.

For example, in the midst of the economic crisis in 2009, one Dongguan factory owner secretly ran off. The local government stepped in to compensate the workers, but they received only 60 percent of the two months' wages they were owed. With wages so long in arrears, workers who had already left didn't get a single cent. Whether workers forgo part of their wages and how much they get in compensation depends on the power and determination of their struggles. For instance, when a Hong Kong owner abandoned his factory in Shenzhen, he had failed to pay the wages of seven thousand workers. The government tried its utmost to stay out of the issue, while the workers complained repeatedly and never got a satisfactory answer. They later blocked a road and turned to the media. Only then did the government show up for negotiations and promise to settle the wage arrears, but workers still only received 30 percent of what they were owed. In April 2011, a factory in Huizhou went bankrupt, and all employees—including all levels of management—took part in a struggle demanding economic compensation. Referencing an earlier case in Shenzhen where employees had gotten double compensation, they exerted great pressure on the employer. As a result, they won one and a half times compensation (according to seniority, each employee received one and a half month's wages for each full year of employment). It is rare for workers to be united in their fight and win compensation. By contrast, workers in small factories that were closed nearby did not get a single cent of compensation.

Compared to strikes during normal factory operation, the struggles of workers during factory closures have some special features. Both cases in part I of this book reflect these features:

1. The workers fight with their backs to the wall. Often they are very active, unified, and show more force than in other labor disputes. The aim of their struggle is clear—for increased wages and it involves a wide range of people—almost all the employees are affected, sometimes including higher management (who are typically more likely to compromise).

2. The factory owner has usually prepared well ahead of time, so workers have limited means to react—even stopping work does not harm the interests of the owner. One shoe factory owner who "did a runner"[1] lied, claiming that he was too busy to take

---

1. Translator's note: *zou lao*, 走佬, originally a Cantonese term for bosses who escape their responsibilities and run away. See: http://baike.baidu.com/view/6137922.htm.

any more orders, and gave the workers a few days off to rest. When the workers came back from their break, the owner had disappeared. For wage arrears, the workers could only turn to the government.

3. In general, actions of workers in closed factories have little impact on the workers in nearby factories. This is in contrast to strikes for wage increases, which can provoke workers in factories around them to take action. When a factory closes down and the local government pays compensation rather than the enterprise, the struggle comes to an end. However, when there is a relatively high number of factory closures in times of economic crisis, that kind of strike can have an impact on workers who are in a similar situation, and workers can use each other's experiences of struggle to gain more power and benefits.

4. Resistance against factory closure can only serve as damage control. Normally, it's hard for workers to get economic compensation from the government. Even if they fight hard, they only win a small portion of what they are owed.

In sum, during this kind of strike workers are on the defensive. In the eyes of the local authorities, even if it is just a fight against a factory being closed, it could "impact social stability." To minimize that impact, many local governments intervene to pacify the workers. As early as 1997, the city of Shenzhen introduced "regulations for protection against company wage arrears in the Special Economic Zone of Shenzhen," which state that companies have to pay regularly into a wage-arrears fund. In case the company goes bankrupt, has to close down, or the owner runs off, the workers' wages are paid out of the fund.

Some years ago, the Dongguan municipal government crafted a wage-arrears protection law, but because of "bad timing" the law was shelved. To this day, no such law has been implemented. In some areas an unwritten rule exists: after a factory closure, the neighborhood committee or the landlord pays the workers 50 to 60 percent of their back wages, but no economic compensation is paid. For instance, when the owner of a leather factory in Dongguan-Dalang ran off and left about a hundred workers with wage arrears of three to four months, the responsible government department offered to compensate them for 30 percent of the wages. The workers were not satisfied and complained to the (higher-up) town administration. In the end, the government ordered the neighborhood committee to pay the workers 50 percent of their wages.

Guangdong Province also developed wage-arrears protection regulations. However, years after their formulation it is still a "difficult birth."[2] Ultimately, we cannot count on rulers to act benevolently and uphold justice. The best method is to act immediately, at the first signs of factory closure. According to my own limited experience and the conclusions of many colleagues, the following events can be forewarnings of an imminent factory closure:

1. *Decreasing number of orders, or outsourcing.* Workers won't have overtime hours; many are dismissed or resign. When the factory is closed down, the owner can save a lot of money in wages and compensation.

2. *Lengthy wage arrears.* In general, companies hold back around one month's wage. If they are continuing to hold back wages, then it is likely that the company has financial problems. In 2009, an electronics company went bankrupt and did not pay the wages of workers or upper-level managers for seven or eight months. The managers failed to anticipate the company closure and did everything to help the owner "get through the difficult times." Eventually, they ended up with their own difficulties.

3. *Fixed assets and raw materials are moved out.* In 2011, the owner of a model kit factory ran off, while the workers were still turning up for shifts as usual. The owner used trucks to take out the molding equipment and raw materials. When the workers found out that something was wrong, they blocked the gate and took turns guarding it in order to stop the boss from further removing machinery and materials and to prevent even bigger losses.

---

2. "Dispute after the Dongguan Government Offered Payments for the Wage-Arrears of a Toy Factory," *Nanfang Ribao*, October 21, 2008, http://city.finance .sina.com.cn/city/2008-10-21/105808.html.

4. *Suppliers turning up frequently to demand payment, or even court officials arriving to confiscate equipment and machinery.* Suppliers demand that customers pay within a certain period. If this payment deadline is not met, they might come to the factory or cut off the supply of goods. If the owner declares bankruptcy, the court can confiscate equipment and machinery. In that case, workers have to be alert and get together to fight for their wages and compensation.

5. *Sudden declaration of holidays.* When, in 2011, workers at a furniture factory turned up for work, they were suddenly asked to take their wages and go on a one-month holiday. In addition, all employees were asked to move out of the dormitories because they were allegedly going to be renovated. Only later did they find out that the owner was preparing to run off.

6. *Frequent dismissals of groups of workers.* Factory owners often use a decline in orders or the off-season as an excuse to fire groups of workers. That way it is not only difficult for the workers to sense anything abnormal, it also undermines workers' solidarity and their ability to protect their interests collectively.

In many cases, workers sense early on that the owner wants to run and will then adopt measures like striking, blocking the gates, or complaining at the related government office. If they can put sufficient pressure on the boss, the workers may be able to protect some of their interests. However, there are sly factory owners who leave no traces when preparing for factory closure or who make feints to deceive the workers. In one case, the Taiwanese owners of a shoe factory in Foshan "moved in several tens of thousands of yuan worth of goods before leaving the factory, so nobody could anticipate that they would run off to Taiwan." In that moment, the workers could only insist that the government "does not shirk its responsibility" and urged the related government departments to compensate the workers for their losses.

Under capitalism, many companies, especially small and medium-sized ones, can suddenly go bankrupt due to competitive pressure. Many factory owners choose to abandon ship. During an economic crisis or in a recession this happens even more frequently. Workers should be mentally prepared, closely watch business operations, and pay attention to any signs that could indicate their factory's closure. In reality, most often, workers have been far too weak to prevent the losses brought about by factory closures, yet it is urgent that we gather the related experiences of workers' struggles and spread them to the best of our ability.

"Closed factory"

Chapter One

Visit to a Bankrupt Factory

Interview conducted June 27, 2010

Factory Background

M Technologies Limited in Shenzhen was founded in 2005. It is a 100 percent foreign-owned company engaged in the development of modern high-tech goods, including research, production, and sales. The main products are headsets for mobile phones, headphones for MP3 and MP4 players, all kinds of earplugs for headphones, multimedia headsets, harness-style headsets, computer headsets, and many plastic components. This information on the company was available on the Internet. The reality is much more complex.

In order to increase profits, capitalists form various kinds of alliances. As Ah Dong, a worker in this company, explained, there are four brothers from Chaozhou who all opened factories in Shenzhen. They use the same company name: M Metal Company. That is the name of the company the second brother's brother-in-law registered in Hainan. It reportedly has a thousand employees there. All four brothers started to run factories as part of M Metal Company. They all order goods under this name, and the products they make are more or less the same.

The factory where Ah Dong works now has another alias: F Factory. As it is still not formally registered, it uses M Factory's name for its production and business operations. F Factory was founded by the eldest of the four brothers, who opened another factory in Dongguan that produces loudspeakers. The oldest and youngest brothers had previously set up a factory in a village of Shenzhen, which they later moved to a town not far away. The second brother earlier opened a factory in S Town. Ah Dong and Xiaonan both worked there until it "went bankrupt." "M Technologies Limited" was labeled on the products of that factory. Up to three hundred people worked there. The third brother not only opened an electronics factory but also a water plant, which also used the brand "M Technologies Limited." In short, those bosses opened factories in many locations and moved them frequently. They even "let them go bankrupt," but this had no impact on their livelihoods. Here, we want to give an account of the closure of the M Factory in S Town.

The Workers

Xiaonan and Ah Dong were classmates in middle school. Xiaonan finished middle school in 2004, just before he went to Shenzhen for work. He was always changing factories or working for six months, then around midyear—the hottest time of year in Shenzhen—going back home. That way he worked half a year, then rested half a year. Six years went by very quickly. In 2008, Xiaonan began to work in the M Factory in S Town as an ordinary worker. He was frequently being moved to different workplaces and often worked in wire tying or the assembly of headphone casings. We did not get any detailed personal information about Ah Dong.

Continuous Labor Conflict

More than one hundred workers are employed at the M Factory in S Town. When business is good it employs three to four hundred workers. The basic wage is 900 yuan, and the overtime wage is calculated according to labor law. The company withholds thirty days' wages as a deposit, and wages are often not paid on time. Sometimes the boss even pays the workers' measly wages in installments. Xiaonan laughed and said that one time the wage was paid in three parts: one part on the first, one on the seventh, and more or less the rest on the eighteenth of the month. All kinds of conflicts and labor disputes arose as a result.

In November 2008, that factory saw its first labor conflict. The cause was wage arrears. The company was supposed to pay wages around the eighteenth, but more than ten days later wages had not been paid. Xiaonan and more than ten other workers went to the labor bureau, but the officials there showed no interest and after a few words sent them away. This made them feel that going to the labor bureau was pointless and they needed to take some "unusual" measures.

Back in the factory, they decided to "try a few tricks." After some discussion some of the workers decided to put on a "jumping from the roof show."[1] A young man from Sichuan volunteered to "jump" and climbed up to the fourth-floor roof of the factory building. At this time, most of the employees were still on the shop floor, working as usual at the assembly lines. None of them knew about the plans to perform the "show." But this action failed to intimidate the factory management. The responsible managers called them "nonsense-talking" and "trouble-making," and they told the security guards to drive workers who stood around back into the workshop. While the young man from Sichuan climbed up to the rooftop, some workers called several government departments (including the labor bureau, the police, and the fire brigade), while others stood by and shouted to attract attention.

Very soon the labor bureau, the fire brigade, and the police all sent staff. The labor bureau told the factory owner to pay the disruptive workers their wages. The boss decided to pay up, but those still working away in the workshop were not as lucky: Their wage arrears persisted. The labor bureau warned the workers behind the action, "You are all making trouble here. You're not allowed to do this anymore!" In the end, that group of troublemakers had no luck either. After getting their wages, four workers—including the young man from Sichuan who had staged the "jumping from the roof show" and three workers who had often been "disruptive and seditious" and had not worked hard—were immediately fired and asked to leave the factory grounds. Still, with

1. Editors' note: Threatening suicide by climbing to the top of a building, bridge, or crane is a popular tactic among migrant workers, as it is a quick and effective way to gain the attention of the authorities.

the wages they received, those workers were happy and left the factory satisfied. Xiaonan was not dismissed, but the event had no positive outcome for him: the managers constantly changed his workstation and gave him a hard time, so he eventually resigned from the factory.

Following the "Jumping from the Roof Show"
The matter had not really come to an end. Two days later, factory security guards staged a "show" themselves for the same reason: wage arrears. Other workers sympathized with the security guards and supported their action: some alerted the police and called several government offices, others attracted attention by shouting, "The company is not paying wages!" and "Someone is going to jump from the building!" Officials from the labor bureau came, and three fire engines plus several officers from the local police station arrived at the scene as well. As in the above-mentioned case, they asked management to pay the back wages.

According to Ah Dong—who still worked in the factory, although Xiaonan had resigned—the factory had six security guards. They were dispatch workers[2] from a security firm and had very low wages. After these events, the security firm complied with the demands of the factory and recalled the six guards. The factory hired eleven people from a "black society" [mafia] to do the security job. One of the guards was really slow. He was the boss, and served as the team leader of the guards.

It was around peak production season, and the factory had many orders. It was so busy that the company had to hire additional workers. The number of employees in the factory reached more than four hundred. However, after the two cases of unrest, the whole workforce was distracted and failed to turn out goods in time. The factory owner was very concerned and invited his managers for a meal, during which he demanded that they handle production with a tighter grip: "What are you afraid of? If anything happens, just ask me. [If the employees don't follow orders] impose as many fines as possible. Whatever methods you use, we need to finish these orders."

2. Editors' note: "Dispatch workers" refer to agency workers who are employed by a third party.

Ah Dong was working as a low-level manager at the time. There was a lot of pressure, so he said to the factory owner, "We aren't meeting deadlines because the workers are distracted, the wages are so low, and you don't even pay them on time. The food in the canteen tastes horrible, and even if we don't eat, food expenses are still deducted from our wages. In such a situation, what are we supposed to do?!"

The owner answered, "I would rather give you money than raise workers' wages." He emphasized once more, "If the workers don't follow orders, fine them as much as possible, until they're left without a dime." Ah Dong told him the lowest-level managers were under too much pressure. "I wouldn't do that even for 10,000 yuan." He feared workers' resistance or that lives would be lost.

The Company Goes Bankrupt

Around May 2009, the company had many orders and still couldn't meet all of them. Customers were complaining and threatened not to give orders to this company anymore. In addition, many suppliers came to the factory one by one to demand money, so the atmosphere at the factory was chaotic. Eventually the factory had no more work, and more than two hundred workers were put on leave. But it was not for lack of orders, since incoming orders were passed on to other factories (most likely including those run by the owner's brothers). The workers had nothing to do and hung around in the workshop. Every day they got off after eight hours. The owner most likely already had plans to close the factory at that time, but in order to save money he did not directly dismiss the workers. Instead, he tried to get them to resign of their own accord—because if he dismissed them, he would have to settle wages and pay severance compensation. On the other hand, if workers were unable to bear the lack of overtime and the major loss of income and resigned by themselves, they would not get any compensation and would also lose a big sum of wages (the factory kept one month's wage as a deposit).

Two months before the company went bankrupt the owner had already "disappeared." Occasionally, the owner's mother showed up to deal with issues. Later, some employees spotted the owner moving some stuff out of the factory, but nobody expected that the factory would be closed down.

Ah Dong mentioned something he considered really funny: the higher managers of the factory, including the vice president, had also not gotten their wages on time. Some even had wage arrears of seven to eight months. Employees would frequently go to the labor bureau to complain about wage arrears, and officials from the labor bureau would often come to investigate. Every time they asked management whether wages had been paid or not, they would say they had been paid. When the factory later went bankrupt and the labor bureau paid compensation, those higher managers confided that they had not been paid their wages for many months. The labor bureau officials did not believe them: "We came every month, sometimes even every week, so why didn't you tell us your wages had not been paid on time?" Because of their failure to inform the bureau, they didn't receive any compensation. Ah Dong said that some upper-level management had a long-standing relationship with the boss, and some had been his friends. So when everything was normal they had taken the owner's side and took special care to protect his interests.

Since the company had always maintained wage arrears, many workers were resentful. One day, Ah Dong and a group of about eighty workers were preparing to take action. At first, the managers were unwilling to go along with them, but in the end they joined the action too and served as representatives to express everyone's demands. When they were leaving the factory, a conflict occurred because the security guards ripped off the employee badges of the leaders.

At that moment, nobody knew what to do next. After much discussion, they decided to go to the neighborhood committee first. The workers complained, "The factory was closed down, and the boss told us to leave." Those in the neighborhood committee responsible for labor mediation said, "Give us three days and we'll contact the factory owner and then get you an answer." They contacted the factory owner, but he had no intentions of showing up in person. For one, he did

he found a girlfriend and was even more in need of money. Together with some friends, he acquired work as a labor subcontractor for a water works project. The wages were alright. Xiaoxi thought that the supervisor, "was not as wicked as other subcontractors." The work gang was made up of more than ten people, and he could earn an average of three or four yuan per day from every worker. After a few years he had earned enough money to pay back the debts of 20,000 to 30,000 yuan accumulated when his father fell ill; by 2004 the debts were cleared.

He had also wanted to marry his girlfriend, but her father did not consent. Xiaoxi felt "girls from the South don't have their own mind. What their father says is all that counts." They had a child out of wedlock. Their feelings for each other gradually changed for the worse, and they rarely spent time together. Xiaoxi had to support the child, and his mother helped take care of the child back in the village. Now Xiaoxi has another girlfriend but has not thought of getting married. "That will come eventually. Right now I am most concerned about my business," he said calmly.

After working as a subcontractor for a while, he did not want to do it anymore because he didn't like the work. He wanted to do some "technical or high-tech" work. More specifically, he wanted to work in an easier and less dirty but better paid job. Xiaoxi's goal was to start a company producing plastic components.

Entering a Factory in the South and Experiencing Worker Unrest

In 2005, Xiaoxi arrived in Shenzhen. First he worked in a ceiling factory as a painter. In 2007, he joined the D Factory, where a strike and road blockade described in this book happened. The factory had a Hong Kong–based owner and was listed on the stock market. It produced goods like electric irons and coffee machines, most of them exported to the USA. In 2006 and 2007, the factory had more than three thousand workers, [but] afterwards the company experienced a slump, and gradually the staff was reduced to only fifteen hundred or so workers. After Xiaoxi joined the factory, he worked two alternating shifts on the hand punch presses. At first, the monthly wage was just 1,500 yuan. Later it increased slowly and reached 2,000 yuan. Once there was a work accident when a male worker of about thirty years of age burned his face after a pressure-induced explosion. The company did not pay him any compensation, so he hung around the factory and received his wage as before.

According to Xiaoxi, the company started to go downhill. One reason was that the management was too lax. For instance, things like packing material were thrown away, and while plastic production rejects can be smashed and reused, the factory management sold the scraps instead of reusing them. It was quite wasteful. Reusing old plastic for production poses some technical problems, and management did not want to deal with it. Another reason was that the company was unable to sustain itself because of excessive debt.

The company did not pay wages and overtime according to the law. Before the company went bankrupt in late 2007, some managers took the lead and filed a collective legal case with three hundred to four hundred workers asking for overtime payments. Several representatives participated in the hearing; several workers stood by and listened. After they won the case, they received only a fraction of payment due. After the bankruptcy, it ended up being the local government that supplied the money. We will come back to that later. From then on, the company calculated wages according to the law.

Forewarning of the Bankruptcy

The factory closed down in October 2010. Starting in September, wages were not disbursed. Every time workers went to ask for their wages, management made excuses—until one day the boss disappeared. Xiaoxi said that before the boss disappeared, court officials had already turned up and confiscated machines, materials (plastics), and so on. Apparently, suppliers had filed requests to secure their property. At that time, they were still producing, but it was thought that the company would not make it much longer. Wages had usually been paid around the twentieth of the month, but from August on they were not paid on time, and then they were not paid at all. The majority of workers had not left because they thought if they continued to work and the company went bankrupt, it would have to pay them compensation of one month's wage for every year [they had worked in the factory].[2]

One day, a manager discovered everyone's wages had yet to arrive and realized the boss had run off. In September, nobody worked anymore, and there were no more big upheavals until the National Day holiday [October 1]. In mid-October, the workers went to the neighborhood committee, but the committee didn't want to deal with it. They went to the labor bureau, but the staff there made excuses, first by saying they would give an answer in three days and later by telling them to start legal proceedings (that is, they asked the workers to file a lawsuit by themselves).

The Boss Runs Off, the Workers Block Roads

Not having obtained a satisfactory answer to their countless complaints, the workers decided to block a road and demand that the government solve the problem immediately. Some worker representatives posted an announcement in the factory, took over the company loudspeakers and shouted, "Whoever wants money should put on work uniforms, and we should go to the government office together!" Twenty-plus workers stayed in the factory to watch over the machines, while more than a thousand walked to the local town government. They held up more than ten banners with such messages as "No money for food" and "We are asking for our legal rights." The main idea was to stress that the owner had run off and they could not afford to buy food. In several-person-deep rows, they formed a long and mighty procession toward the town government.

The road leading to the factory was completely blocked, so no car could pass through. The workers only allowed one driver to pass when he said his wife was in the hospital giving birth. The drivers were cursing the workers, but they replied, "You need to shout at the government, because they haven't paid our wages and they don't care about our situation." The mayor came in person and said that the government would solve the workers' problem as soon as possible. A person from the labor

---

2. Editors' note: This is the correct calculation for severance pay, according to the Labor Contract Law.

inspectorate used a loudspeaker to shout that everyone should turn back and that the government would deal with everybody's problems. A foreman bought five or six packs of mineral water, and everybody sat down on the road, drank water, and ignored the shouting man.

Since they feared the workers would make more trouble, four buses with riot police turned up, each bus with forty to fifty cops. They went to the government [building] as a "protective escort." When they arrived, they bought a carload of mineral water and brought it into the courtyard of the government [building]. The workers had been walking for more than three hours and were tired, so they all went in and drank water. Once they entered, the government [officials] started negotiating with them. The workers' demands included: (1) payment of the wages the company had not paid for several months, including overtime; (2) payment of compensation. At first, the government asked the workers to file a legal case. That would have taken at least a month, so the workers declined. Then the government asked for three days' time, so they could announce their search online for the factory owner; if the owner would not return, they would pay the wages. They also promised to pay the workers 300 yuan for food expenses the following day. The workers said that they were hungry and wanted to eat, so the government agreed to buy them food, but afterwards they were taken back to the factory in travel coaches and did not get anything to eat.

The Workers' Representatives Negotiate

The five workers' representatives at that factory were all skilled personnel or managerial staff. They were not chosen through elections but were people the workers generally knew well and trusted. All of them had worked in the factory for more than two years. Interviewees said that they felt the actions and words of the representatives during that strike were in line with everyone's interest, and the workers trusted them a great deal. For instance, at the beginning there were only thirteen hundred workers on the company's list of employees, but the representatives included all the workers who had already returned home. In the end, they successfully fought for wages and compensation, and informed those who had already left to come back to collect. When the representatives had to take care of some tasks and needed money, each worker contributed 5 yuan. Those five representatives were primarily responsible for negotiating with the government. Everyone expected they would find an immediate solution in the next day or so, but in the end the representatives gave the government three days' time. After they stopped blocking the road, the government wanted to negotiate with the workers [again], and, as usual, asked to speak with the representatives. The workers were generally unsatisfied and had doubts that the representatives would be able to take care of things. One representative felt wronged and said he would quit.

The next day, the government came to the factory and provided some money for living expenses as agreed the day before. "A lot of media came then, like the Pearl River Channel (Guangdong TV), the Business Channel (CCTV), First-on-the-Scene (Shenzhen TV), and Fenghuang Satellite TV. Afterward many TV stations showed the scene of the government officials handing out money for living expenses. The government looked heroic." However, the workers were less than satisfied, and one woman commented, "How far can we get with 300 yuan? We buy a bag of rice, and that's it. Vegetables are so expensive now."

About one week later, the government posted a notice in the factory, announcing that compensation would only be 30 percent [of what they were owed] and there would be an assembly that evening. During that assembly, the town government, the labor bureau, and the local police—more than ten people—discussed the problem of wages and compensation. Several hundred workers came, all of whom lived in the factory. Those living outside the factory did not know [about the assembly] and did not come. The government made advance payments for all the wages and overtime, but it did not want to pay all the compensation. They complained, "The boss ran off, and the government has no money." In truth, the 300 yuan for food expenses paid before, the wages they gave to everybody, and the compensation, all came out of the wage-arrears protection fund. There were some older colleagues with a lot of money at stake who were firmly opposed to this and were finally led out by public security personnel. The next day, after 10 a.m., [the workers] could sign an agreement to receive compensation.

At first, everybody was resistant and refused to sign. The representatives were the first to agree to sign, saying, "this is our only option." Afterwards, some cowards signed. We can suppose that those who signed first were bribed by the government. Initially they had vowed to fight for compensation, yet now with such little compensation offered, they immediately took the lead in signing.

When Xiaoxi went back that night, he checked online and saw many websites had covered their story. Some people said they admired the workers, which made them proud. Meanwhile, other companies nearby were closing down, but those factories were small, and all resistance was suppressed. The government was prepared to pay back wages, but there was no severance compensation.

[Years earlier] in December 2008, the factory of Xiaoxi's girlfriend produced loudspeakers and other electronic goods and employed about a hundred workers. It went bankrupt, but no compensation was paid. Those workers fought for and won some compensation, which is rather rare.

Some Conclusions

The day of the demonstration, a lot of media outlets turned up, among them some foreign media. Fenghuang Satellite TV was the first to report on the factory closure. Shenzhen TV did not dare to report it and left it out of the broadcast. All the workers felt Fenghuang Satellite TV was good, since it broadcasted the facts. After they entered the government courtyard, the workers demanded that Fenghuang also be allowed to enter, as they had covered the factory closure before and were useful in the workers' eyes. The government had no choice and agreed to their demand. An interviewee said the government responded so fast to the demands not because of the workers themselves but because the media's presence increased the pressure. Asked why they chose to stage a demonstration against the government, he said, "We never believed the government, so this was to put pressure on the government to pay us wages. However, the government always delayed and tricked us."

Before Xiaoxi's factory, other factories had already closed down. Xiaoxi observed that the companies showed the following indicators before shutting down: no orders, no overtime, wage arrears, the boss suddenly going on holiday, then the secret removal of machines. Other factories closed down without showing any forewarning. For instance, before B Factory, the G Factory went bankrupt. Staff were removing everything from the factory, and there were no TVs, computers, or such things anymore. Later, the government took everything back. In G Factory, there were absolutely no forewarnings of closure.

On the issue of factory closures, Xiaoxi said, "It is necessary to prevent suppliers, the court, or anyone else taking the machines." When the boss ran off, he owed suppliers several million yuan, and the [unpaid] workers' wages amounted to eighteen million yuan. The machines had a value of more than ten million, and included a new injection-molding machine imported from Japan that alone was worth more than one million yuan. Everybody was thinking, if the government doesn't pay the wages, "we can sell the machines to pay the wages." At the time, some older employees suggested (not too seriously) that the workers should take over the machines and start production by themselves. Everybody thought that sounded like fantasy: "The suppliers have not received their money, the factory is in a mound of debt. How could we get it off the ground?!"

Part II: Struggles against Wage Cuts

This part includes ten worker accounts of strikes against wage cuts. The term *wage cuts* is used here as a general reference to the reduction of workers' income—including benefits and allowances. Bosses have many methods to deal with workers; they don't necessarily just cut the basic wage. In fact, especially when they are forced to comply with increasing minimum wages, capitalists often abolish benefits. Increasing work intensity without a change in wages, the shifting of rest days to avoid overtime payments, increased fines, as well as arrears and embezzlement of wages are other tricks bosses often use.

This part includes interviews with ordinary strike participants (from chapter 3 to chapter 7) as well as interviews with workers who initiated strikes (from chapter 8 to chapter 12). For easier reading, we have separated those two types of accounts and analyzed them separately. Each section starts with an introduction written by Hao Ren.

Section One: Ordinary Strike Participants

Most people we interviewed for these strike cases were ordinary participants. Though they were not leaders, they still were under considerable pressure by the boss to return to work. The activists faced the most pressure. Almost every manager will secretly seek out the organizers and target leaders, core [workers], and activists. Tactics include directly isolating and firing them, or enticing them, using them to "win over a portion of the people," only to transfer them to other posts or fire and blacklist them later. The capitalists might, at the same time, put pressure on ordinary strikers and divide them in an attempt to break through the weakest line of defense. The methods used are not necessarily scolding, threats, or violence. Managers might be sent to the workers, demanding a return to work, asking the workers' representatives to negotiate, using nice words to buddy up to them, or even inviting them for a meal.

In fact, in these cases there were no leaders, or if there were any, it was hard to call them "organizers," even if they actively organized a large number of workers or consciously planned and carried out the entire strike. In general, the strikes broke out when the capitalists suddenly reduced wages, cut benefits and allowances, or introduced new rules unfavorable to the workers, like not granting overtime or unreasonably shifting rest days. The most common form of strike occurs when workers receive their wages and realize they got less money than they should have, and all decide to "quit working" without prior consultation. That is a spontaneous act of defense against a capitalist attack. As for conscious strikes, for instance, when experienced employees use their networks to spur on a group of workers to strike, or when skilled workers and low-level managers mobilize a section of the workers, the degree of organization often [still] remains limited. Many workers participate not as a response to the mobilization or the call [for action], but because they "see that other workers aren't working, so they also put down their tools." Widespread dissatisfaction with working and living conditions has caused many strikes. Even if only a fraction of the workers initiate the strike, they still easily attract the sympathy and participation of other workers. If the workers make a secret agreement during the long hours of production line work—especially on a covert slowdown, an agreement on the collective reduction of the work speed—the strike will take shape more smoothly.

However, when the boss and the authorities "ask the workers to select representatives for negotiations," the weakest point in the workers' struggle becomes obvious. Due to the lack of preparation, workers' demands are often not collectively and systematically formulated, so it is easy for the bosses to muddy the waters. A worker said about his strike experience, "When we go on strike, whether we negotiate or not is not the most important thing! It's most essential to stick to a fixed wage demand and believe that our collective strength can defeat them." The initiators [should] put forward a full set of demands and discuss and revise and add to them with the help of workers, or they [should] directly draft approved demands after discussing with workers, with a strategy of "fixed wage demands," thus helping all workers to set a clear goal for the struggle and to follow it to the end, not returning to work until the aim is reached. If not, capitalists can use negotiation over wages to separate workers and representatives, because some of the workers or representatives might think, if the capitalists "make that concession, that's already pretty good," and will then be unwilling to continue the struggle, leading to the loss of fighting spirit. This strategy [for workers' struggle] is especially suitable for the strikes without representatives often seen in the past.

In fact, there is always the fear that "the bird that pokes its heads out will be shot." Workers' consciousness is not at the point that allows them to call a worker assembly to elect representatives, so strikes without representatives are quite common. The strike in a Japanese-owned factory for the payment of a high-temperature bonus in 2010 was a typical case: since the strike was completely unorganized, there was no core of workers and no plan, and the ad hoc proposal (to block the street) was prevented by the police. The workers "gradually dispersed" and eventually "everyone sought out familiar faces, and the feeling spread slowly that it made no sense to carry on." Though there were plans to continue the strike the next day, "security pushed everyone who turned up inside, and they could not gather." Nevertheless, it needs to be stressed that a strike that lacks organization and preparation might still enable workers to win certain benefits. What's more, workers' will to resist can be stimulated, and they might learn useful lessons for the future.

If the workers elect representatives as soon as the strike starts, these representatives will most likely become targets of vigorous attacks by capitalists and the authorities. So even if the strike has a core and organization, it is still better to have "reserve cadres" that can take the lead without going public. That way it is possible to continue organizing and to maintain the struggle after an attack by the capitalists. This is the best method to prevent the capitalists from repressing the strike, and [only] when negotiations cannot be avoided should workers publicly "elect representatives." At this point, the risks for the representatives are relatively small.

During a strike in a toy factory in Dongguan the following happened: the workers of a nearby factory had been on strike and blocked the road. "The police came and demanded to talk to the representatives. The ten representatives came and were dragged away for beatings." The toy factory workers learned from that, and when the police came during their strike and asked the workers to choose representatives for negotiations, the workers refused, saying, "Each person represents only their own interests." It is not hard to imagine that as soon as workers' consciousness and fighting spirit reaches a certain level and they set up forms like strike committees or representatives' groups as structures of leadership, state suppression intensifies enormously. At that time, a mutual relationship between the workers' representatives and ordinary strikers has to be deliberately established; that is, the workers' representatives have to be backed up and controlled by the collective force of the strikers at all times. That helps to gain the upper hand during negotiations with bosses and officials, and can prevent internal divisions and compromises or sellouts by representatives. During the struggle, workers should ensure that the boss won't try to "settle accounts later."[1]

For instance, during a strike in an electronics factory in 2002, even though they had "self-selected and mutually nominated" workers' representatives, "after the representatives had been chosen, the other workers slowly dispersed until it was impossible to exert any collec-

---

1. Editors' note: that is, fire worker activists.

tive pressure during negotiations." After the event, there was no stable workers' representation mechanism that could have protected the activists, so the leaders were first appeased, and [later] the bosses "fired them one by one."

While pressure on strike leaders is relatively intense and hard to evade, ordinary participants feel both pressure (fear of retaliation or of being fired) but also "excitement." Suddenly they are rid of the daily drudgery, restraint, and humiliation, and by causing some trouble for their oppressors, the thrill of revenge and a rebellious spirit spontaneously arises (although maybe they feel to some degree that "one should not take part in making trouble"). In addition they get the chance to relax physically and mentally. In a situation where they cannot effectively organize, many strikers take the opportunity to take some days off and rest, to "finally get a breather." But workers frequently fail to participate in the struggle and lack "awareness" of the strike, and don't have significant thoughts and dialogue about the aims of the struggle. That makes it hard to continue the strike; the strength and the effectiveness are greatly reduced, and many ordinary strikers don't get a full or profound sense of participation out of the struggle and don't increase their awareness and militancy. That has happened not just in a specific case in this book but, in fact, is a phenomenon that can be observed in many strike situations. When a strike has just started, it may "bustle with noise and excitement like a festival celebration," but if the bosses or the related government offices have the means to delay the matter or exert constantly increasing pressure, the group of workers will most likely be dispersed. In addition, since the aim is unclear, strength cannot aggregate and [the strike] ends in confusion, depression, and exhaustion. In fact, only by taking one action after the other (for example, road blockade, demonstration, collective petition) can these problems be temporarily avoided.

As some workers we interviewed said, "At that moment the strike spread out to the streets . . . for those kind of actions you need relationships and connections, you have to wait for the busy season of factory production, then you have a [strong] position in negotiations"; "the female workers stood around and in the front . . . protecting the core colleagues" (because "at that time, many strikes happened in Shenzhen, and all workers knew, during a strike, the male workers would get into fights with the police and could be arrested; on the other hand, the police did not dare touch female workers"). These experiences were passed on by word of mouth, and they are very valuable. It makes sense to summarize, analyze, refine, and disseminate these experiences in order to support workers' learning process and progression from spontaneous resistance to conscious struggle as soon as possible.

Chapter Three

A Strike Demanding
High-Temperature Subsidies
in a Japanese Factory

Interview conducteded August 6, 2011

Xiao Mei was born in Hubei Province in 1985 and is a mother of one. She and her husband are working in Shenzhen, leaving behind their son in their hometown. After finishing her second year of high school she went to Dongguan where she worked as a general laborer, quality control (QC) operator, and quality clerk. Now as a general laborer in a factory of household products, she also works part time for a marketing firm called Wanmei.

Up until now, she's worked in a few factories. Previously she found that each time she moved to a new factory they would offer higher wages. But this time she took a pay cut, making it seem as if the former factory (the Japanese factory where the strike happened) had the high-- est wages (3,000 yuan per month). So why did she leave the better-paid factory? Xiaomei was concerned that she had been there for three years but had never been able to change her position. She didn't want to be a low-level manager because she thinks it's a thankless task to supervise workers who might get annoyed, not to mention her lack of such experience. Xiaomei said that she got all the experience she needs to do this work in the first factory she went to (in Dongguan). Within just two years, she had learned a lot in different positions like QC and quality clerk. These positions were somewhat easier and freer than the common assembly-line jobs and were not as high pressure. A general worker might be evaluated based on both quality and quantity; however, a QC operator is only responsible for the quality and could walk around after finishing her job. And, with some subsidies, the pay was better than for general workers.

We heard that Xiaomei had been involved in a strike in the previous year so we invited her for an interview. To avoid misunderstanding, she emphasized that she was not an organizer and didn't know why the strike broke out—that she was just passively involved. She didn't see any future in working in these factories and she wanted to realize her own value and be recognized. She saw dissatisfaction within the factories, viewed the confrontations and the strikes as "negative" actions, and didn't want to talk too much about them. Probably because she wanted to get rid of such "negative" things, she could barely recall how the strike happened, even though it was just one year ago. However, she did show a little excitement when she talked about the strike.

The General Situation in the Factory

Located in an industrial park outside the special economic zone in Shenzhen, the Japanese factory where the strike happened had thousands of workers as well as a branch factory. The branch factory Xiaomei worked in had four or five hundred workers and manufactured precision products like mobile phone keypads. The main factory produced household electronic appliances. The two factories were not far away from each other, sharing canteens and dormitories.

There were some bad things about this factory, including the difficulty of trying to establish a relationship with the managers and problems with bribery. Though she was offered a monthly wage of 3,000 yuan on the basis of her three years' work experience, Xiaomei didn't want to go back to work in that factory unless she could transfer jobs. It's hard to get a promotion, though there was a lot to be learned in the factory. The high-level positions were all occupied by the more senior workers. She once had two job interviews for a position of a document handler, but finally failed (as had other interviewees) because the position was supposedly given to a factory insider who had personal connections. Bribes of 1,000 to 2,000 yuan to the management were necessary to be hired as a technician. You also needed to take the bosses out to dinner. The bosses would come to dinner with friends and relatives, often accompanied by some "hot chicks" they found in the workshops.

Coercive male-female relationships were rampant here. People with official titles had lots of mistresses from the factory. There were some benefits for the mistresses, such as easier job positions, higher wages, and easier access to promotions. Sometimes the women really had feelings for the men, but the men were just having fun. It's not hard to understand the situation since there were more women than men in such factories. People were no longer surprised by such things.

The Causes of the Strike

One cause of the strike was the cancellation of the high-temperature subsidy. According to J, there had been high-temperature subsidies for years: 100 yuan per month for indoor workers and 150 for outdoor workers. In July 2007, the high-temperature subsidy was abolished because, according to the factory, there was going to be air conditioning inside the factory. Another cause was issues with wage increases. The general workers' base salaries were raised in July 2007 in accordance with the increase in Shenzhen's minimum wage. However the middle-level workers—QCs, technicians, and small managers who didn't benefit much from the raise—were dissatisfied about the limited wage increase and the narrowing wage differential with workers. The monthly wage gap between the middle-level workers and the general workers had been about 400 to 500 yuan and it was reduced to about 100 to 200 yuan after the adjustment.

When payday arrived in July 2007, the cancellation of the high-temperature subsidy for the general workers and the narrowed salary gap between the middle-level workers and general workers became the immediate triggers for the strike in the main factory.

The Strike Process

From Xiaomei's perspective, the strike seemingly came out of nowhere. That day she went to work as usual, but stopped at the factory gate where she found lots of workmates gathering without any intention of going in. She was told that there was a strike and no need to go to work. There were about two or three hundred people staying at the gate, mostly day-shift workers with only a few night-shift workers. When asked whether she was afraid to have her salary docked, J said she knew there would be no deduction of salary because the strike would certainly be effective since everybody was participating.

The managers above the level of section supervisors were all Japanese and they didn't talk to the strikers face to face. Instead, they told the management staff to pass information on to the strikers. After waiting at the gates for about half an hour, the Chinese managers came out to talk with them. Xiaomei couldn't remember exactly what they said, but the basic point was to get them back to work. Nobody seemed to actually listen to what the managers were saying. The workers were shouting, "We will never go inside unless our demands are met." And the voices that burst out included diverse demands for an increase of the night-shift subsidy, complaints about the limited increase of wages, and even complaints about poor food. A variety of different views were heard all over the place with only one point of consensus—no returning to work.

The strike involved all general workers and some middle-level workers, but no high-level managers. It was started by the night-shift workers who asked the day-shift workers not to go inside the factory at first, which is when a crowd began to gather. Later more and more people (probably the night-shift workers who had just punched out) joined the crowd surrounding the factory gate. Different opinions emerged when it came to the means of bringing pressure to bear on management, including suggestions of blocking the B Road (a main transport route in this region), calling local TV stations, protesting in front of the local village government, and so on. Some workers were quite hesitant and people became divided. Later the traffic police and security guard brigades showed up and stopped the rest of the people from heading to B Road, while some others were already on B Road. At this point, some workers threw out the idea to mobilize the workers in the main factory. The security guards didn't manage to stop these workers, and they ran into the main factory's gate and called their workmates to come out. However, they were blocked in by management.

Later, the labor bureau sent two officers. A protective cordon was set up by dozens of police and security guards to surround the strikers gathered at the gate, leaving just a small opening for going in and out. The road in front of the factory was blocked by the massing crowd. However, since it's a remote place within the industrial park with little traffic, no big problems resulted. At 10 a.m., the officers from the labor bureau asked the strikers to elect some people to represent the workers' views and to negotiate with management. But nobody volunteered. The strikers insisted on talking collectively without being represented, for they feared that a single representative might not have the fortitude to defend them as a whole. Management refused to talk with the entire group, so they were at an impasse. The labor bureau's attempts to coordinate didn't achieve any results. There was no definite viewpoint agreed to by all strikers and it was chaotic; everybody was indecisive and just following the crowd.

Feeling tired after being on their feet for a long time, the strikers ran to the nearby cultural center to sit down. The night-shift workers didn't go to the dorm to sleep. Later on, lunches arrived for the strikers, though they had no idea whether this was provided by the government or the factory. Nothing much had changed by lunchtime when the workers inside the factory left to eat. Those workers had half an hour for lunch and some of them just came out to have a look and then left. There were some slight differences in wage adjustments between the main factory and the branch factory. Perhaps things were not as problematic in the main factory, so those workers didn't join the strike.

The security guards who blocked the strikers from going inside to mobilize other workers in the morning were more relaxed by midday. So the strikers went into the factory to use the toilets and get drinking water. Without the general laborers at work, managers were sitting in their air-conditioned environment and chatting. Xiaomei gave a good loud laugh about this and said, "We were all burning in the sun and they enjoyed air-conditioning inside." The managers understood that they also stood to benefit if the strikers were victorious, so they didn't take action to halt the strike or demand that they return to work. The strikers came back outside after they got water to drink—everyone knew that the strike would be meaningless if they were inside the factory.

Two TV vans appeared after someone called the media, with a man and a woman in each. They interviewed workers about the process of the strike, the demands of the strikers, and management's response. Some workers made comments, but the journalists didn't seem too enthusiastic about taking any risks, and the story didn't end up getting any coverage.

In the afternoon, basically nobody else came by. The strikers were tired and sitting on the ground, with people from management standing around. The traffic police closed the road leading to the village government to prevent a protest there. By 2 or 3 p.m., people began to stir and talk about protesting in front of the government offices. After Xiaomei got back from the toilet, she found the first batch of more than ten strikers already on their way to the government. The traffic police were very frightening and it was only possible for a few strikers to stealthily break through the blockade when they were not watching. Some were chased. It was rumored that someone was arrested and taken to the police station for violation of some law, so nobody else dared move. Even though they had broken the blockade, the strikers who had intended to go to the government changed their mind, while the others just stood where they were. The crowd began to disperse with more and more people going back to the dorm. By 5 p.m., nobody was paying attention to the strikers, and nobody sent dinner. The strikers went to the canteen to feed themselves. By evening nearly all the strikers disappeared and then the traffic police left as well.

Resuming Work and Results

After dinner, some workers went to punch in then came back to sit outside. Some hung out in front of the nearby shops, and some went back to the dorms. Just then, the director of each division came to

overtime. The only positive feature of the job was the cheap boarding provided by the factory. The living expenditure at that time was about 150 to 200 yuan, which was directly deducted from their wages. Xiao Lan only kept enough money to cover her living expenses, and sent all of the rest back to her family in the village.

The overtime work was excessive, and workers had to work until very late every night. Working overtime until eleven o'clock in the evening was normal and sometimes even until one or two o'clock in the morning during a busy season. Xiao Lan and her workmates all looked forward to Sundays and other holidays, because on Sundays no overtime was required and during holidays they were allowed a day off.

Just how exhausting was the work? Xiao Lan recalled that one night she had just finished overtime and was busy writing letters—at that time, workmates usually wrote letters to each other since cell phones were not yet popular. Writing letters was how workers communicated and expressed their feelings. She must have fallen asleep for she did not wake up until 11 o'clock the next morning due to the accumulated exhaustion. She was roused by the ruckus when some workers entered the dorm to install electric fans. Xiao Lan had to keep quiet and pretended to be asleep when these male workers came in. Since many other workers were about to have lunch after work in the morning, she could not go to the shop floor to work. That half-day off was counted as absenteeism. However, she luckily was not penalized because management was not very strict and the reward and penalty system had yet to be specified.

The Management System

The employees in that factory had six ranks: assembly-line workers, line assistants, line managers, foremen, supervisors, and factory manager. Each foreman supervised two to three assembly lines, each line with forty to fifty workers, one to two line managers, and two to three line assistants. Line assistants usually took charge of chores, substituted, and helped line managers to arrange work. They also worked for production workers if the latter went to the restroom, and thus they were relatively closer to basic level workers. At that time, it was obvious that workers remained antagonistic with line managers who often verbally abused them. In general, the relationship was bad.

Workers remained kind to each other, chatting, gossiping, and complaining about wages, benefits, and management when they were not overwhelmed by the work. Female workers had strong ties with fellow villagers and old classmates, and they often got together after work. Workmates usually talked to each other on the shop floor or in dorms.

Before and After the Strike

On the Eve of the Strike

The strike took place in June 2002. Xiao Lan didn't know anything about it beforehand. It was a Sunday and wages has just been paid. Xiao Lan returned to the dorm with her workmates after shopping and heard people talking about "going on strike tomorrow." She was suspicious about the credibility of this information, because it was not rare to hear of plans for strikes in this factory, especially when there was a lot of overtime and people were exhausted. However, usually it turned out to be nothing more than idle talk without any real action. Nevertheless, Xiao Lan still felt somehow excited. The following day, she was looking down from her dorm room and noticed that many people had gathered by the basketball court. She now became more excited, given that she was quite dissatisfied and exhausted after a lot of overtime work. This time, words became reality.

Xiao Lan recalled that the dorms at that time had no hot water. Workers had to fetch hot water on the third floor, and the whole dorm building had nine floors so going up and down stairs was exhausting. However, it was the lack of wage hikes that directly triggered workers' anger. The wage increases were differentiated according to job positions. Moreover, the pay increased too slowly, much more slowly than the rising cost of living. In the previous six months, wages had either not increased at all or had only gone up by 0.5 yuan per hour.

Strike Leaders

The strike was initiated by the machinists in the machine shops. Later, some line assistants were also very active. They were paid 1,100 to 1,200 yuan per month, higher than the unskilled workers, but not by much. Their overtime rate was the same as the one paid to the unskilled workers; the only difference was the basic wage. On the eve of the strike, these line assistants printed some leaflets that listed workers' grievances, including low overtime rates, excessive overtime, no hot water in the dorm, poor food in the canteen, and so on. All of these issues were near and dear to workers' hearts. They distributed these leaflets to every dorm and encouraged others to join the strike.

The Strike

The factory had staggered schedules for workers to arrive in the morning, with groups arriving at 7 a.m., 7:30 a.m., and 8 a.m. On the day of the strike, Xiao Lan was scheduled to start work at 7:30 a.m. Workers who started at 7 a.m. went into the workshops as usual. The strike leaders and workers scheduled to start at 7:30 a.m. all gathered by the basketball court. As time went by, more workers gathered. After seeing the strikers, some workers who had already punched in came out of the workshop to join the throng.

At that moment, a large number of workers started to march on the road, which was immediately full of workers wearing the same outfits. The destination of the march was the township labor bureau. The machinists who led the march walked in front and pulled out a banner, but Xiao Lan could not recall what it said.

Xiao Lan said there were many strikes in Shenzhen at that time, especially in foreign-funded electronics factories. Prior to the strike in her factory, two strikes already took place in the neighboring factories and it was popular among strikers to march in public.

Xiao Lan also followed the march, but she was not sure where the labor bureau was located or what would happen next. Some police came to ask where the workers were headed, and they responded "to the labor bureau." The police pointed workers in the wrong direction, but workers unanimously ignored them.

The whole march had two to three thousand participants. As the march came upon an industrial park, a large number of traffic police, public security officers, and riot police were called out to encircle the workers and block all the road entrances and exits. Workers started to consider how to break the blockade, and shouted, "charge this way!" Other workers joined in in trying to break the police cordon, but ultimately they failed. One female worker was shoved to the sidewalk and asked the police to send her to the hospital and to apologize; otherwise, she refused to stand up. Workers were inspired and gathered to support her. Though the situation looked unstable, there were only minor physical altercations.

The male strike leaders were consciously pushed to the core or the back of the crowd, while female workers stood in the periphery or in the front. Many female workers who used to be docile and obedient on the job became very brave and militant; they stood in the front to protect the male strikers.

This strategy emerged from recurrent strikes in Shenzhen during that time. Workers were aware that male workers were more likely to be arrested if they confronted the police, while female workers were relatively safe given that police would not dare touch them. (Female workers would scream, "Harassment!" if they did.) For this reason, they devised a way to arrange women in the front and outside to protect men in the center.

Later on, the labor bureau and other "related" departments—strikes usually concerned all government departments, but Xiao Lan was not sure the specific ones—sent out officials, along with foremen, supervisors, and other management personnel, to speak to workers. They succeeded in sowing divisions among the workers. Their main goal was to persuade everyone to return to the factory to negotiate with management.

Xiao Lan recalled how ridiculous management was at that time. One supervisor in the administrative department attempted to persuade workers to stay inside by saying, "Look, it's too sunny. Please go inside so you won't get sunburned. Also we have so many orders to fill . . ." One foreman beside him echoed, "Indeed! Feel free to voice your concerns when you go back. We can definitely have a discussion." Xiao Lan could not help laughing when mimicking their speeches. She said it was so ludicrous that they still responded like that when a strike was already going on. At that time, one female worker stepped forward, shouting at them, "Is there any use voicing our concerns? The wage was only increased by 0.5 yuan for the last half a year and our overtime pay was only 2.5 yuan!" She went on to speak out about other grievances, and was warmly applauded by the others. People all started to put forth their complaints given that their dissatisfaction had accumulated for a long time.

More than one hundred officials from the labor bureau also joined the efforts to persuade workers to return to the factory. The two parties were at a stalemate for hours, during which time workers could not leave while factory management and government officials could not get in. In the end, management asked workers to send representatives for negotiation. Workers responded in unison, "We're all representatives!"

Nevertheless, this did not help solve the problem. Workers eventually selected five to six people to negotiate. The workers trusted these representatives, who were chosen from among the line assistants and machinists who initiated the strike, as well as some unskilled workers who had worked in the factory for a longer time. They were not selected by formal elections but by self-selection and mutual nomination.

Negotiation

Once the representatives had been selected, all but one or two hundred workers gradually dispersed. After the negotiations ended, the worker representatives came out to let the others know the results and the factory also immediately posted notice that it would:

1. raise the base wage to 480 yuan in accordance with the Labor Law;
2. start to deduct the meal cost (previously free) from wages after the pay increase;
3. cancel the year-end bonus (50 yuan per year) and full-attendance bonus (30 yuan per month);
4. increase the water and electric deduction from the wages.

In sum, the pay increase workers succeeded in struggling for would be eliminated by the new deductions. Workers were certainly not satisfied and complained about the results.

The factory created one mechanism, the bimonthly staff representative congress, for workers to express their opinions about work. Two representatives were supposed to be selected from each production line, but in reality they were not democratically elected. Instead, one of the two representatives was always the line manager. Xiao Lan was once asked to be the other representative for her line, but she became extremely disappointed after attending a meeting. She found that only supervisors, office clerks, line assistants, and line managers talked continuously while ordinary assembly workers never had a chance to speak. Not only could grassroots workers not report their concerns but they also had to listen to the quarrels and mutual complaints among the managers. For instance, if one line manager asked for an improvement in his or her benefits, the others would respond by saying, "Your situation is bad, but ours is even worse." They couldn't reach any unified demands. Managers were only talking to each other, which was not helpful in solving any real problems. Everyone got frustrated after the meetings, which proved to be nothing more than a formality and a public relations show.

After the negotiation, a couple of machinists who were strike leaders were appeased, but later the bosses fired them one by one. Some of them left with "negotiated discharge of labor contracts" and were granted economic compensation. Some left because they did not want to renew their existing labor contracts. Others were simply fired. All of these strike activists gradually left the factory. But the line assistants who participated in leading the strike were not influenced, and they kept their jobs.

Analysis

Along with the wave of strikes in Shenzhen, two strikes also had taken place in the neighboring factories and both factories had to immediately increase their employees' wages. These successful cases had a positive demonstration effect for the strike in Xiao Lan's factory. Workers became more confident when they witnessed the actual benefits brought about by the strike.

Most factories nearby were foreign-funded electronics factories and many of them were quite large. When asked why strikes usually took place in large and foreign-funded factories, Xiao Lan said, though large factories typically had better legal compliance, and offered higher wages and better benefits compared to their small counterparts, the latter relied more on kinship or friendship networks to recruit workers. Because of the personal ties, it was more difficult to have a strike in small factories if there was no activist to take the initiative. Sometimes, even though collective struggles did happen, they were more likely to be undermined by relatives or friends of the factory owners snitching. Therefore, resistance in small factories was more likely to be initiated by managers.

The factory where Xiao Lan worked paid hourly wages. Line managers took control of the speed of the entire line. Nevertheless, during the ordinary assembly work, workmates naturally developed a sort of tacit agreement. Xiao Lan and her coworkers would pile up the parts when they could not finish assembling them as an expression of discontent and non-cooperation. Especially when the line manager was absent, Xiao Lan would take the initiative to ask all workers on her production line to slow down. When inspectors came to record time, workers would also slow down. Sometimes, Xiao Lan tossed products around the shop floor to express her dissatisfaction. Veteran workers were usually more daring than the new ones. Those workers who wanted to leave but could not get permission would also intentionally slow their work pace to try to provoke dismissal. The concerted efforts to slow down gradually became a good practice for the line workers to form solidarity and to collectively express discontent. This kind of tacit agreement played an important role in later struggles.

During this strike, hometown networks did not play a significant role. The strike was triggered by the workers' longtime discontent about the poor working conditions, the high-intensity labor, and the low wages. It was initiated by the relatively skilled workers and low-level managers, and was supported by the other workers. Though networks among fellow villagers did exist, they were not a crucial factor in this strike.

The strike had no detailed arrangement or clear plan in advance. Although the machinists distributed leaflets to encourage this collective response, ordinary workers, including Xiao Lan, were not informed at all about the planning process. The actions on that day—starting from going on strike to marching on the road and negotiating with the factory management—all depended on the circumstances at that time, rather than following a well-made plan by workers.

Personal Opinion and Experience

After participating in this strike, Xiao Lan felt very excited and happy. So she looked forward to the next strike, realizing that striking could bring real benefits to improve the living conditions of workers. She previously tried other channels to express discontent, for instance, by submitting complaints to the staff suggestion box, but never got a response. In comparison, organizing workers for a strike could bring immediate effects and also demonstrate the collective power of workers. Nevertheless, Xiao Lan does not regard this strike as successful, given that their wage increase was offset by cuts to benefits.

The key to the failure of the strike was that the workers didn't understand the importance of negotiation. When the factory management set about to divide workers, workers' sense of solidarity was too weak. People were somewhat indifferent when selecting representatives for negotiation. Most of them only thought of the strike as a day off for rest or to have some fun but didn't pay attention to the process or the content of negotiations.

Learning from this strike, Xiao Lan suggested that workers shouldn't disperse but should instead gather together and continue to exert collective pressure during negotiations. She also felt it was important for workers to pay close attention to and understand how representatives negotiate, as well as the content of negotiations.

"Good news: you're getting a raise!" (left side reads: food deductions, water, and electricity deductions, bonus reductions; right side reads: enterprise boss)

Chapter Five

A Strike Triggered
by Wage Arrears

Interview conducted May 2, 2010

Gao is a worker who started his life as a migrant worker in 2007 (before that, he had stayed on the farm back home). He had worked for several factories in Dongguan and the strike he took part in happened in the second factory, which produced toys. Having heard early in 2008 that the working conditions were better in Shenzhen, he moved there and became a team leader working for a Korean factory.

The First Experience of Working Outside

It was Gao's dream to work hard and devote himself wholeheartedly to work when he first left his hometown for Dongguan. He was attracted by an advertisement for a position in Plant A (with tempting promises of high wages and short working hours) and started working there. The boss was from Jiangxi Province, and he had 6,000 to 7,000 workers and about five hundred security guards working for him.

Payment

The general base salary for low-level workers was 900 yuan per month, with a maximum of 950. There was a deduction of about 150 yuan per month for food and living expenses. Gao found this treatment "acceptable," but overtime wages were not paid according to the

Labor Law standards. The overall monthly wage was between 1,200 and 1,300 yuan (by inference, the hourly overtime wage should have been 3 yuan).

There was a so-called registration fee of 50 yuan that was supposed to be returned to the worker after three months of work. Gao was suspicious whether the money would be returned or not. He asked, "How the hell do I know if they'll give it back or not? They just said they would add it to the wages."

Orientation Training

"It's like brainwashing," said Gao. It's required that the workers should love the factory and work passionately. The workers even had to learn a factory song.

Timetable

A queue had to be formed at 7:30 a.m., followed closely by singing the factory song. At 7:45 a.m., workers entered the workshops. There was an hour for lunch and half an hour for supper. They were off work at 9 p.m.

Strict Management Measures

There was "standardized management," which has been characterized as military-style management. For workers, it's like living in prison. Security guards were there to enforce all of management's decisions. Workers "belonged" to the boss and "there was nothing the guards couldn't do." They were more or less like "instruments of violence" (Gao's description) for the factory. Gao described two related conditions:

1. Dining: There was a canteen where the workers had to eat together under the supervision of the guards. No talk was allowed at the table and no leftovers were permitted. Workers had to be careful not to drop any grains on the floor when they filled their bowl with rice, or they might be taken away by the guards to receive a lesson. They could also be forbidden from eating any more for that meal.

2. Zoning: Of the six zones dividing the whole factory, Gao stayed

in Zone Two, which had about two thousand people. The six adjacent zones formed a circle. Gao marveled at the factory's brilliance for this kind of geographical layout, for if anything happened, the guards could quickly besiege the workers and bring things under control. Gao described a worker from Henan Province who couldn't bear the factory and left. After leaving, he gathered a group of his hometown friends to exact revenge on a security guard who had treated him badly. When they found the guard, they surrounded him and beat him.

Due to the "outrageous" behavior of the factory, worker turnover became an issue. Again management showed its brilliance and coercive force. When it came to workers quitting their job, management was nothing but obstructive. It was very hard for the workers to get management's agreement to allow them to resign, and almost impossible for a worker to leave his job freely without medical documentation. A "retained" sum equal to forty days' wages would be deducted if the worker didn't get the factory's agreement to resign.

However, Gao was able to successfully resign. By hounding the manager daily for a week without affecting his work, the manager finally approved his resignation, but asked him to keep it a secret. Gao explained that he refused the manager's offer to quickly promote him to be a team leader (with a monthly salary of about 1,400 to 1,500 yuan) during his application for resignation. He was quite satisfied about his legitimate and successful resignation, especially in comparison with those who had to leave automatically without getting back their deposit, either because they were afraid of making trouble or of the guards.

Thus, right after his resignation from Plant A where he stayed for four months, Gao started work in a toy factory, Plant B, where the strike happened.

The General Situation in Plant B

Gao's impression of Plant B was that it was "even more outrageous." He cited two points: first, the food in the canteen "wasn't fit for humans," and it cost them 200 yuan per month; second, it was almost impossible to ask for a day off even for illness. What's more, a worker would be fined 200 yuan for one absence from work (think about the ratio to the monthly salary). Other situations were quite similar to Plant A: the base salary was about 900 yuan, and the factory held a deposit of forty days' worth of wages.

Gao also mentioned that Plant B consisted of groups of workers mainly from places like Guangxi and Yunnan Province, totaling more than two thousand people. Because the actual conditions in the factory bore little resemblance to the advertisement, there were two batches of three hundred to four hundred workers from Yunnan Province who left the factory, under the leadership of "headmen" (we didn't inquire about the details, feeling Gao might not know them). The headmen were a kind of broker between the workers and the management, who had their own special interests. On the one hand, they took a commission from the factory for bringing in workers; on the other hand, they had to protect the interests of their fellow villagers.

The Strike

The most outrageous and unacceptable thing in this factory was the payment of wages. Gao said the payment method was quite chaotic, particularly in the bonuses, which were determined randomly by supervisors and ranged from 50 to 100 yuan. The monthly wage for a supervisor often exceeded 10,000 yuan. Because of the low wages and meager benefits, the fines, and withholding of wages mentioned above, the lower-paid workers were quite discontented.

The workers had gone to the labor bureau many times before the strike took place, and the official reply was always We'll look into it, but it takes time. "We surely can understand it if they need to investigate. But we felt something was wrong when they didn't move an inch the whole time," said Gao. When legal action was unsuccessful, some workers began to consider striking. "There were 3,000 or 4,000 workers in another factory that produced toys not far away. The strikers fought back and even blocked the national highway. . . . Later the police showed up and asked representatives to negotiate. And the representatives got beaten up," said Gao.

Representatives from different factory departments initiated the discussion of the strike, and also encouraged the workers and organized meetings. At the beginning, more than a dozen workers from Henan Province felt an impulse to rush into the office building with steel pipes, but Gao calmed them down. The representatives consulted the workers the evening before the strike and confirmed there were three hundred who committed to take part. The actual number of strikers was less than two hundred the next day.

The strike lasted from 7 a.m. to 10 a.m. Instead of going to the production lines, the two hundred or so workers gathered, demanding to negotiate over the salary system. The security guards showed up to preserve order and the two sides faced off. "Management steals our hard-earned money," shouted a worker standing on a table. The supervisor went angrily to beat him but was stopped by the workers, who surrounded him and threatened to fight back if he made a move. The supervisor had to give up.

Eight men were sent by the local police to demand that workers elect representatives. But the workers had learned from others' experience, and rejected this demand on the principle of "everybody representing his or her own interest." The officers from the local police station left the factory after asking for some information and having expressed their inability to take any action. One of the police said to the workers, "It really is messed up in this factory. As long as you guys don't stir up trouble, we won't intervene."

The workers had contacted local media, so the local newspaper came to report on the strike (which, according to Gao, was the workers' main approach to fighting management). Finally, forced by the situation, the factory made some compromises. Many workers left the factory immediately when they got their deposit money. Gao left the factory after three months.

Some Observations

Wait-and-See Workers

Some workers agreed to join in the strike while some were afraid and went to work as usual. But workers in some other workshops began to follow the example after a degree of victory had been achieved in the strike, which allowed the unrest to sweep through the whole factory.

Powerful Supervisors

The supervisors, especially those from key departments like the "Hot Glue Division," had great power and good salaries of about 2,000 yuan per month. The supervisors had major influence on the appointment of staff, so their departments were often staffed by fellow townsmen or other people with whom they had a good relationship. As for team leaders, since they were usually technicians, their attitudes toward the lower-paid workers varied. The owner of the factory was a military veteran. He had some political identity as "Chairman of the People's Congress."[1]

Work Experiences Afterward

Having worked in a toy factory with more than a thousand workers for free for seven days, Gao realized that all the local factories were "basically the same." He later went to five or six factories in Dongguan. Gao was not the only worker who moved around a lot, as quitting was common. Workers are excessively exploited by the factories through wage deductions and deposits. Besides, these factories were characterized by hardship, bad treatment, and insecurity. For example, Gao once worked for a computer components factory. After just half a day of wiring electroplates, his fingers began to swell up.

In 2008, Gao went to Shenzhen when he heard from his workmates that the environment was better there. He paid 250 yuan as an

---

1. Editors' note: Local People's Congresses are the legislative bodies in their respective administrative areas. No further details about the official position of the factory owner were available.

introduction fee in order to work for a Korean company. "There are still good bosses," said Gao, "though maybe less than 20 percent of the total." Local labor laws and regulations were generally adhered to by the foreign factories (usually just exactly at the minimum level): the hourly overtime wage was 8 yuan on a normal workday, 10 yuan on weekends and 15 yuan on holidays. "The laws are okay; the problem is primarily about legal enforcement. There could be a win-win situation." When some passerby said, "The Labor Law is only for protecting the rich," what seemed to be a disbelieving smile passed over Gao's face. For now, Gao stays in the factory as a technological team leader in charge of two or three production lines. Like when he first left home to work, he remains positive.

Chapter Six

A Male Worker's
Two Strike Experiences[1]

Interview conducted April 9, 2010

A Brief Individual Introduction

My brother was admitted by a university in 2002 with a yearly tuition of more than 10,000 yuan. My family had just built a house then. My father tried to borrow money everywhere, but nobody could help. I was forced to drop out of school and stayed at home. Later my uncle asked a friend of his who was a manager in Dongguan to bring me out to work.

July 29, 2002, was the day I left my hometown and arrived in Guangdong Province to start my work life. Of the thirteen people making the journey, ten were girls. We were all from the same county. Each of us paid an introduction fee of 400 or 500 yuan. We felt so happy at that time because we had really longed to see the outside world when we were at home. First, we thought it's liberating to have some space away from home; second, there was a feeling that it's respectable to work "outside"—those folks who worked in Guangdong Province were the envy of the village when they were back at home. They dressed themselves in fashionable clothes and had hundreds of yuan in their wallets. Some even had mobile pagers, which were quite prestigious.

---

1. Editors' note: Chapters 6, 7, 11, 12, and 14 were written in the first person, while many of the others were written in the third person. Despite being inconsistent, this is how it appears in the original.

We had never thought about the bad aspects like workplace injury or occupational disease before. Our fellow villagers who worked outside only spoke of good things when they returned. And I only understood later that everybody buried the pain in the bottom of his or her heart to prevent their family members from worrying. I was once mugged and my wrist was injured, which made my family members really worried. They demanded that I come home during the spring festival holidays whether I had money or not. And they would send me money if I didn't have any. So after that I never spoke to my family again about problems to keep them from worrying.

The First Strike

When I arrived in Guangzhou, I carried a big woven bag to cross the Liuhua Pedestrian Bridge. A driver took my luggage and threw it into a bus, then brought us to the J Electronics factory in Dongguan. This factory produced pocket calculators, and it's one of the five or six Chinese factories owned by a guy from Hong Kong.

I only had 100 yuan left on me after I paid the introduction fee. My brother had given me 50. My first meal was fried rice noodles and it was delicious. The factory housed me in a very old building, with seventeen other people sleeping in bunk beds. The aisle between the beds was only half a meter in width. There was a bucket for collecting leftovers at the gate of the dorm, and it smelled terrible. The showers were above the toilets; it was really filthy and stinky.[2]

The food in the canteen was gross. Once the steamed rice was found to be too raw to eat, so three or four workmates from Shanxi Province carried the rice barrel into the manager's office. We all followed them. They dumped the rice on the desk of the manager. They cursed the manager, complaining that while they could bear poorly cooked food, they couldn't handle a raw meal. The manager later bought each of them a bag of instant noodles. We felt so happy about this. For the next

---

2. Editors' note: In China, many toilets are "squatters." It is not uncommon to have the shower head directly above, so that the toilet doubles as a shower drain.

few days, a little bit more meat appeared in the dishes. The rice had been really foul, since they used diesel as fuel to steam the rice. On the spring festival menu, there was a dish of "stir-fried pork with ginseng" (actually it was stir-fried pork with radish), which everybody was really happy about. The food in the special canteen for management was rather good, with abundant fish and meat all day. We sometimes ate the leftovers brought by a fellow villager who was a manager.

My job was to attach the chips to the conductors on an assembly line. My hands were in pain after my first day. The work day was from 7:30 in the morning to 12:30 in the morning. There was lots of overtime and sometimes we even had to work all night. During the spring festival period, I had been working nonstop for forty-eight hours from the twenty-eighth of the twelfth month of the lunar calendar.

I was paid 9.5 yuan per day with 1.15 yuan per hour offered for overtime pay. There was hardly any break time during most workdays, and only a day or two off a year as a holiday. The toughest time for me was when I ran out of money to buy things. My biggest desire was to eat as much as I wanted when I got my paycheck. My first forty-five days' worth of salary was withheld by the factory, and all I had on me was the 50 yuan that I had borrowed. I later became disgusted after having eaten only instant noodles for a month. The first salary I received was 89 yuan (my salary for eleven days). I could hear the beating of my heart when I had it in my hand. It was a thrilling moment when I got paid for the first time.

Working in that factory I could save about 200 yuan a month. And my record was 500 saved after deductions for food. So that made it possible for me to send about 3,000 yuan to my brother in college at the very beginning of the year.

The main causes of worker resistance were low wages and arbitrary fines. You could be fined 100 or 200 yuan for a tiny infraction. The salary, which was only about 300 yuan, could be reduced to zero after fines. Management would curse out workers and then demand an apology from them. Nonpayment of wages was common. Wages were supposed to be paid on the fifteenth of the month, but were frequently delayed by several days, leading to worker resistance.

The strike I was involved in was also caused by unpaid wages. Workers were prevented from going to work by some senior workers at the gate that day. Having seen several senior workers taking the lead, the personnel manager asked them to resume work and promised there would be something delicious for them to eat later (noodles with pork). Those senior workers were quite familiar with each other for they had been working in the factory for a long time. Other workers saw them blocking the gate and stood there watching. It seemed really fun and I thought, "If they don't go to work, I won't go to work. After all, I hadn't had a break for such a long time." The action wasn't referred to as a strike since everybody was just focused on getting their money immediately. The managers called the team leaders and assembly line supervisors to get their workers back on the line. I thought it was kind of awkward to go against the manager who was a fellow villager of mine, and began to think about resuming work. My team leader made token moves to call us back to work without really pushing. The factory threatened us, saying that it's our business to decide to stay or leave since it would be easy for them to get new workers.

I was a little bit worried about being fired due to the fact that it's harder for a male to find a job and there was very strict policing of temporary residence permits,[3] so keeping the job became my biggest goal. Instead of going to work, I went to watch TV with some other workers that morning. Strikers from the same assembly line got together and complained about the hard work.

A notice was posted that day asking the workers to wait for two or three more days as the factory's bank account hadn't yet received the money. The notice convinced some to return to work; however, some others went to the dorm and resumed work only in the afternoon. The situation was finally resolved when we got paid after two or three days. Since our factory wasn't the worst, everybody was relatively satisfied.

---

3. Editors' note: In the early 2000s, it was still not uncommon for police to demand to see migrants' residence permits. Without employment, they could be detained and "deported" back to their villages.

Leaving the Factory

Out of the thirteen folks that came to Dongguan, only four remained. I was reassigned to the warehouse because my uncle called my manager and asked him to take better care of me. It was very hard work, and I was paid 300 yuan per month and had to go on business trips quite often. I disliked the work pretty strongly for its bad pay and sometimes sneaked into the warehouse to sleep until 10 p.m. when I was not that busy.

I talked to the manager about getting a promotion. But there was no precedent of promoting a general laborer to a management position and it's really hard to get a raise in that factory. So I resigned and was rehired again with a new fake ID. I got a better offer of an additional 1.5 yuan per day and 0.1 yuan more per hour for overtime. I was still not satisfied with that and eventually resigned. The rule then was that a worker who resigned couldn't be paid off immediately and he had to find a "helper" to get the money for him later after he left. The "helper" got a cut of the money (100 or 200 yuan). I "sold" my last two months' salary to the manager for 900 yuan, of which he took 200.

The Second Strike

In 2003, I successfully interviewed for a position at J Electronics.[4] The interviewer only asked about where I came from and my work experience. She hired me because she thought I had clean hands. A kind of electronic belly band, which could be wrapped around the waist to generate heat, was the main product and was sold to European and American countries. The boss was a member of the Kuomintang.

The environment here was much better than the other factories. I was happy to work since there was a water heater in each eight-person room. After only three days of work I had earned my first salary of 200 yuan. The job was much easier than the previous one. Management

---

4. Editors' note: Both factories in this narrative are referred to by the same name in the original. But based on the account, they are clearly distinct factories.

even provided us with hot milk if we had to work overnight. There was a daily morning meeting, which usually covered quality issues and the production situation. I came on time when I was new, but eventually started showing up late.

My job required that I pull threads of electronic blankets with a workmate. We had to finish thirty threads in an hour and I could finish sixty in two hours, after which we could relax. There wasn't much overtime. The latest we got off work was about 10 p.m. It was rarely necessary to work overtime through the night.

A year's stay in the factory turned me into a senior worker. I didn't have any contract or insurance then. In June and July 2004, we were so busy trying to meet tight deadlines that we didn't have a day off. Sometimes we were completely exhausted by working overnight one day after the other. A team leader, who was a fellow villager of the manager, continuously increased our production targets. It later increased to two hundred pieces a month from the previous one hundred. The team leader had timed us with a stopwatch when we were producing at peak speed, and then used this to set the new quotas. We then had to meet these new targets. People sometimes fainted from overwork. We all wanted to send the team leader of the workshop packing.

There was an ultrasonic department just next to our assembly line, and their job was to use hot glue to attach two layers of cloth together. I did wiring work with a number of old workmates of mine. They complained about the tough work and talked about leaving. Later they came out to lobby us to drop what we were doing and expel the team leader. We then stealthily spread the word about striking, but one of the team leader's buddies leaked the news. We agreed to get together after work at Yijia (a supermarket).

We had lunch, took a nap, and got up, then changed our work suits before we went out. But we were stopped at the dorm's gate by the team leader who challenged us and asked us to get dressed and head to work. He was put off when I told him that we were going to work. After he left, about forty or fifty people went to Yijia. Management couldn't stop us. Some workers on other assembly lines also stopped work when they heard about our action.

As we were talking at the entrance of the supermarket, ten people, including the manager, clerk, team leader, assembly line supervisor, and material handler, all showed up to bring us back to work. We all dispersed immediately. Later a senior worker we knew well called us to gather in Lingzhi Park, and about thirty people showed up in their work suits. That's where we wrote a petition addressed to the factory and signed our names. But some didn't sign it for fear of being fired. Our primary goal was to expel the team leader. We were all of one heart then and even mentioned in the petition how we didn't have labor contracts or insurance.

A clerk called to ask where we were, and we said that we were in the park. The manager drove to the park later to persuade us to resume work, and we dispersed again. Some went shopping, some did their laundry, and some slept in the dorm. Having seen us not working, the workers at the new factory also went on strike that evening. We senior workers set an example for them.

The assembly line supervisor who was in charge called a meeting at Yijia to inform us that the factory was going to fire us. The old factory also had a strike the following day. Everybody just went to hang out. The big boss came from Taiwan on the third day when we were just having fun at Jiangnan Department Store. The boss brought about sixty of us to an open field. He asked us to elect a representative and tried to buy us off with 20 yuan each. Nobody moved because we thought there was no possibility that we could be bought off with 20 yuan. The boss said, "Is it that you mainlanders can't be bought off by 20 yuan?" We ignored him. More than ten people went to his office as he later requested. He wrote down our demands and promised to send them to the headquarters in Taiwan to be dealt with as soon as possible. And we were promised a monthly gathering where they would provide cake. In the afternoon, people were still scattered. I went to the workshop to check if there was anybody working. The manager who found me later said, "When you're away from home you have to depend on your friends. If you ever need to borrow money, just ask me." It sounded totally fake to me.

A notice was posted promising all problems would be resolved in a week. I went with three other workmates in the manager's car to search for other workmates to get them back to work. Later on, some workers got a good dressing down by the manager in the office of the old factory. The manager said, "If you have anything to say, put it in the suggestion box. Don't create trouble. Us coming to the mainland to open a factory is good for local economic development."

We resumed work the next day. After a week we signed a contract with the factory with an increase of base salary from 580 yuan to 590. We were provided with overtime payment in line with the Labor Law, as well as insurance coverage, and there were some improvements to the dorm. Later on, we could get a monthly salary of about 2,000 yuan, better than the other factories nearby. We strike leaders were blacklisted and assigned to different positions without being fired. I was originally supposed to become an assembly line supervisor after several years of work, but this didn't happen. Other things remained the same. The team leader of the workshop we wanted to expel stayed around, and we had to meet his production quotas.

There was a security guard who had urged others to sign the petition during the strike. However, he disappeared after he got some financial compensation, and some workers were not happy about that.

A Few Thoughts

I think the relationship among the strikers was rather good. Being united, the brunt of the strike was directed at the management. Somebody called the labor bureau, but it was useless. People with strike experience told us that there was strength in numbers and nothing could be done by a single individual. The participants were not concerned about any consequences. With no previous experience, I didn't know it was a "strike," and just thought we would stop work. No one was specifically persuaded to join. It was voluntary and the representatives emerged organically. The core was mainly the senior workers of about the same age who had stayed for a long time and had networks that helped to bring people together. When the strike ended, we were basically satisfied. We would still choose to strike if all this had happened again. We have more experience now. Any action like this requires a strong interpersonal network. Our bargaining position is better if the strike takes place during a period of peak production.

The strike succeeded for two reasons: the boss was nervous because of the tight deadline (the last batch of goods was sent by air instead of sea) and the workers were familiar with the factory.

After the strike I worked at the factory for more than a year and then left in December 2005.

Chapter Seven

An Electronics Factory Strike in 2005

Interview conducted November 12, 2010

I come from Hunan Province. After being in high school for one semester, I left home to work in 2004, as my family had had a tough time after buying a house in 1996. My mother got sick in 1997. My father ran a brick kiln together with my uncle, but the kiln was shut down after my uncle got put in jail for some reason. Many relatives left to work in construction, so my father followed them and some fellow villagers to work for a road construction project. After working for one year, however, he didn't receive any wages due to the financial crisis. My uncle on my mother's side was the subcontractor, and he didn't get any money either. Neither did the person who gave him that contract. My uncle gave my father 1,000 yuan, 500 yuan as my father's salary and 500 as a gift. We wouldn't have survived the Chinese New Year without that money. My uncle then brought a bunch of workers to find the boss's car and they jacked a tire, so the boss ran for the hills and hid in a shabby house. My uncle just wanted to scare the boss, but my father was so angry that he beat the hell out of him. The boss was hospitalized and he came to our house asking for compensation during Chinese New Year. Others thought it was my father's fault, that he was just being over the top. After that, they didn't bring my father with them when they went out looking for work.

We didn't have too much farmland. My younger sister was born in violation of the birth control policy, and we didn't have enough food to support the family. My mother was allergic to pesticides and therefore wasn't able to do too much work on the farm. My older brother was good at school, but he stayed in a high school nearby so he could help with spraying the pesticides. His teacher understood, given my family's situation. Because we didn't use pesticides, a huge proportion of the rice we harvested was hollow and we had to borrow rice from other families. My family's economic situation was just so bad. My older brother and I were in debt to our school for tuition, too, until a relative working in the school promised to waive the fees.

When I was in my first year in high school, my brother got admitted to a university in Changsha, majoring in mold design. My family thought that boys should pursue higher education, so they wanted to support my brother. My academic performance wasn't that good, so I was the one to quit.

Getting Recruited for the First Time

After leaving school, I found it hard to find a job, because I didn't have a network and therefore lacked information about where to go. A cousin of mine had left to find work earlier, and his uncle happened to come back home at that time, so I left the village with that uncle to go to Shunde.[1] When I saw factories on TV, they always seemed so nice: well-built buildings, tiling, and a clean environment, so I thought it should be fun. It would be a decent thing to do. I had this thought in mind at that time: I will make money and become successful, as long as I work really hard.

The factory was not hiring when I got there. I lived in a basement with my cousin and his uncle and aunt. There were three single beds separated by curtains in that basement, which accommodated three couples and their children. In the summer, the couples slept in the beds and the children on the floor. They worked in a textile plant,

---

1. Editors' note: a city close to Guangzhou.

so they were able to steal clothes from the factory—that's why we had curtains and sheets. I stayed and ate in that place during the day. After dark, my fellow villagers secretly brought me into the factory. There were three rows of dormitories for girls and two for guys, each row with more than ten rooms. The dormitories were one-story metal houses and it was so hot in the summer. Most workers lived in the factory, while people with families might rent a place outside. There was no fee for the dormitory, and no manager, so you could change rooms whenever you wanted. People not working for the company could enter the factory and live there as well, if they could borrow a uniform and employee ID from someone.

I waited for half a month until the recruitment period started, and I got hired. I still remember a stupid question I asked during the job interview. "Are mosquito nets provided here?" I asked. The interviewer rolled his eyes. "Why don't you just ask for an air conditioner? I have been here for years and I've never heard about the company giving mosquito nets."

At that time, I had a plan for my own development. In the first two months, I would learn the procedures at every work station; by the end of the third month, I would be familiar with everything. I also wanted to do quality control in half a year, and become a line leader within no more than one year. Then I got into the factory and things turned out totally differently. The plant looked nice. I had never lived in a multi-story building, so it felt exciting to climb the stairs and be upstairs. But the machines on the shop floor were dirty, and the work was tiring. It was just such a huge contrast. In the beginning, things were very tough. I cried from time to time when calling home. My mother wanted me to go back to school, but I thought it was already impossible.

Basic Information about the Factory

The electronics factory, hereafter referred to as "H," was located in L town, S city. It produced fans for engines, rice cookers, and microwaves. It's just by the freeway, so you arrive the second you get off the bus. There were six-hundred-some people employed by the factory, mostly female. I arrived at H Factory in the summer of 2004, and the strike happened during the Dragonboat Festival of 2005, shortly after which I quit.

The payment system was a "collective piece rate." In the first two or three months I was just a sophomoric newbie without any "rank," so my wage was only 450 yuan a month. 90 yuan was deducted from the 450 yuan for the meal plan. I was a growing teenager with a good appetite when I first arrived, and needed triple the amount of food for every meal. Fried rice noodles for breakfast was 0.5 yuan each, and I needed three orders. The highest wage I earned was 630 yuan.

The longer you stay, the higher your rank. Workers were ranked by line leaders; and the line leaders' favorite people would get promoted faster. My factory was pretty nice—my cousin was there for more than ten years until he became a line leader and saved enough money to build a house back home. After the factory closed, he moved to XL town.

We had a lot of orders then, so we barely got any days off all year, except National Day. We worked at least twelve hours a day, usually from 8 a.m. to 10 p.m., sometimes till midnight, while occasionally starting work earlier when we had to rush an order. The three rows of dormitories had seven or eight restrooms, and the shower was in the restroom as well. Restrooms were always crowded at night, so we had to take turns. What's more, we usually got so exhausted after work that some people took a shower at dinnertime and gave up the meal.

Before the strike the highest wage I got was 630 yuan. Other people could get as high as 800-something. Line leaders made about 1,000 yuan. Work was tiring, and we would engage in some intentional sabotage. We would secretly bring our meals to the shop floor, and put some oil and salt on the products, so they would rust easily. We would also put in some trash, sunflower seed husks, or hair when packing the products. This was mainly to vent our anger. Managers and the boss could not be on the shop floor at all times, and there were so many people wrapping and packing that management couldn't figure out what was happening in this chaos. After delivery, the customers might find problems in the product without knowing how to deal with it, so we would be sent to them to fix the problems. We traveled for this reason to Dongguan, Shenzhen, and Humen[2] and found it fun.

We couldn't leave our seats to walk around at work. There were cases of people dying from excessive overtime. But people rarely knew about it, because that happened during the night shift. Whether there was compensation is unclear. Then people became afraid of working in that workshop. They were scared. Another person died in the dormitory and the company gave that person's family 130,000 yuan. People thought the boss was nice. Another coworker ended up in a vegetative state after being hit by a car, and the driver ran away. The company asked us to donate for the coworker. We thought the boss was so stingy, asking us to donate while he himself was making so much money. But we showed our solidarity by donating several thousand yuan. This number looked impressive given our low wage. My brother's[3] uncle said that workers were very involved in donating, and many people visited that person in the hospital. That person wasn't very amicable with others, but we felt bad about this kind of thing anyway. People were very sympathetic. I felt sad when hearing this, too.

A Mini-Struggle

We frequently had to use chemical thinners. In the beginning we didn't know it was toxic, so we used it to remove paint and clean the floor. When the weather was hot, we put it on our bodies. It smelled bad but felt cool and comfortable. My feet got badly inflamed and I don't know if it had something to do with the thinner. I stayed in my bed for a week with a fever. I asked for sick leave. My supervisor was a fellow villager of mine, but she was mean—I learned to curse in this factory. She said, "What do you think you are? A prostitute? Asking for a day off while working away from home?" We had a big fight and

---

2. Editors' note: a township within Dongguan municipality.
3. Translator's note: This is likely the interviewee's cousin, as she mentioned above, whose uncle brought her into the factory. Kids growing up in the age of the one-child policy often refer to their cousins as brothers or sisters.

I wanted to quit. She didn't listen to me so I decided to talk to the boss. The managers' offices were not in the workshop, but in the office building with security guards. I took off my uniform and entered the office in street clothes so that I would not be stopped by the guards. I ran all the way to the boss's office, but felt scared when I got to the door. The secretary said that the boss wasn't there and asked me who I was looking for, so I said I was looking for a manager. I talked to manager K about the sick leave thing, and he seemed to be on my side. He made a call to my supervisor and asked her to give me a day off, saying this was a trivial thing. I felt the manager was nice and full of human warmth.

The Strike

It happened around the time of the Dragonboat Festival in 2005, on the twenty-fifth I think.[4] That's pay day. Originally the company said they would pay us in the morning, but they had just adjusted the wage for my line and knew it was too much for us to bear, so we didn't get paid until 4:30. We got off at 5:30, so there wasn't time for us to discuss anything after receiving our payment. We knew that our wages were too low. We did the same work as other lines, but earned 100 yuan less than those workers. Our supervisor was the same age as me. We thought that her relationship with the managers was not that good so she wasn't able to fight for our interests. We frequently saw the foreman criticizing her, saying that she didn't manage us well, and she cried.

Other lines had already received their wages, and we were the only ones still waiting. People started to chat and speculate about what might be happening. We stopped working at 2:00 p.m., but nobody came to us to explain the situation. So we just stopped. At 4:30 p.m. we got our payment and found it as little as we had anticipated. Someone said, "Let's not come in to work tonight." People agreed, although we didn't discuss it beforehand.

---

4. Editors' note: The Dragonboat Festival takes place on the fifth day of the fifth month of the lunar calendar. This date refers to June 25 on the solar calendar.

The more than forty people on our line didn't check in to work that night. We dined in the hotel across the street, which cost 20 yuan per person. That was a lot, but everybody went. No one stayed behind. It was easier to talk there because we were not on the shop floor anymore. We said the managers might find out who suggested that we stop work. Someone said that anybody who snitches would be a lowlife. Many people talked about their grievances—some stout folks like me and two other workers, five or six longtime employed men and several eloquent women. Everybody was cursing. Worried about having nothing to say, we collected our grievances and requests. Since I was keeping notes, I contributed many points on that list, but I asked people not to say they were from me. The next day, I wrote down all the requests on a piece of paper and we all signed the back. I also left a blank space in case someone came up with other requests. There was a place for the manager to sign as well.

We talked about what we should do in the afternoon since we were not going to work. We agreed to go out and have fun, and return to the dormitory after the managers left work. So we went to the park and riverside. It was fun because it had been a long time since we had last visited those places. Then it started to rain and there was no place to go, so more than forty of us just went for a stroll. We were all in our uniforms so the passersby wondered what we were doing. We went to the apartment of a female coworker. All forty of us and three or four of her family members crowded in that place. We drank a little bit and fell asleep. We also talked about what to do the next day, and someone suggested that we should visit a temple.

We started thinking about the next step when the rain stopped. We lived in different dormitory rooms. We planned to switch dormitories with some coworkers so we could stay in two rooms next to each other, with two or three people in each bed. If management came by, we could respond together. We also discussed who the spokesperson would be if management wanted to talk. We thought that we should be together for any event.

Our supervisor wasn't involved with the strike at all. When the workshop manager found her, she was knitting. She argued that her attendance on the shop floor was meaningless anyway, as there were no workers there. After we got back to our room, she brought the workshop manager to my room. They were mean from the outset, threatening me by asking if I still wanted my wages.

I had been in the factory for a relatively long time and was familiar with all the procedures, so I frequently substituted for other people. It allowed me to walk around on the shop floor, which was fun. One time, when I was picking up material, I saw a piece of paper. It said that the order we were working on was due on a certain date, and that there was a penalty if the factory couldn't make it. So we knew that what we were producing was due very soon, and they would beg us to work if we didn't listen to them. The manager was mean to us, but we didn't pay attention to her. So she tried to be nice, saying that the factory would treat us nicely. But we didn't buy it. We hid in our blankets, held our noses, and said, "Bullshit." Walking around the room, she tried to figure out who had said that, but couldn't. Then she started crying. She said that she was a worker as well. It was just her job to persuade us to go back to work. We didn't feel any sympathy, and asked her where she was at the beginning. After all, she didn't come to solve the issue when we stopped working. We always wanted to yell at this woman. She always dressed like a man and liked to chat with pretty girls. The workers said that she was a pervert behind her back. A male manager went to the dormitory for guys, and he failed to convince them, either.

We went out the next day, because we were worried about being investigated by management. Someone might get scared and confess. We met at the ceremony hall and left together. The supervisor somehow learned where we were to meet, so she waited for us there. She told us to be careful and not to be too extreme. The boss is a local, so we have to watch out for our safety.[5]

That morning we went to a park, as some people didn't want to pay to eat out again. A manager made a call to our supervisor and asked her to find us, so she called the materials receiver from our line. Only she

---

5. Editors' note: The implication here is that the boss might have connections with local gangsters.

and a few other senior workers had cell phones. The supervisor asked about our whereabouts and what we were doing. We kept super quiet when they were talking, worrying that she might abandon or even betray us. If that happened, everything would be over. She was very loquacious and cunning, so we didn't trust her and were worried. Some people whispered about taking her cell phone away, but nobody acted. The supervisor said that she wanted to meet. We were afraid that she might bring "people from society,"[6] which could be dangerous. But then we decided she probably wouldn't so we let her come. She bought us a meal and about seven or eight people—all of them more aggressive, angrier, and more determined—came along. The supervisor gave us some suggestions about how this thing could end up. She also told us some possible strategies of the company to deal with this strike. We said that the immediate reason to strike was wages, so she explained why the wage was that low for that month. We then said it had always been that low, so she stopped talking. We guessed that the supervisor was probing us, trying to find out who the strike leader was, rather than coming to tell us the company's strategy.

The supervisor said that the manager was inviting us to a hotel for dinner. We said that we shouldn't go unless we all go together. But some people were scared, and some others didn't know what to say. Plus, the supervisor said it was impossible to have everybody go together. So after we discussed it, about five or six people went. Upon our arrival, we saw our "little boss" and two managers. "Little boss," L, was originally an engineer, but ended up joining the owners and became a boss. The two managers were from the marketing and production department. We drank a lot—several cases of beer. But we only had made small talk without touching on anything important. L and the managers tried to build a relationship with us. Little boss asked me where I was from, so I said Hunan. He then announced that he was from the same province as well—he was actually from Jiangxi. He was good at talking and bragged a lot that night. I said that I didn't drink, but the supervisor said it's

6. Editors' note: This likely refers to gangsters.

impolite to refuse a drink when L was toasting. I secretly poured the alcohol on the floor. When we drank enough, L said that since we had had fun and had been able to rest, it was time to come back to work. We said that we had to talk to the others. They asked us what in the world we wanted, and we said we had to discuss it together. We promised, however, that we would go back to the shop floor and discuss there.

The atmosphere changed when we came back to others. They were suspicious about the possibility that we sold out to management. Some people began to waver. We said, "Now we cannot sleep separately." We told them all the things we talked about during the dinner. Several older people were still suspicious. The third day, when we entered the workshop, nobody came to negotiate with us. Maybe the managers thought that the problem was over since we drank so much. The workshop manager started the line, but we shut it down once she left. She asked who did it, but we didn't answer. She asked why we wouldn't work, and we said we were waiting for the manager to talk to us. He came after an hour and talked to us. There was a very tough and aggressive woman, whom I called "big sister," in our group. She was illiterate, not even able to write her name, but she was really eloquent. She spoke in an extremely convincing and understandable manner and used metaphors and examples. She didn't attend the dinner with managers for fear of making mistakes, but now she was very talkative. She listed our demands, and the manager agreed to some.

1. No morning shift.
2. At least one night without overtime after pay day, so we had time to deposit our money in the bank. We meant to ask for a day off, but we found it was not realistic.
3. Better food. We wanted to have meat. The manager said that the canteen was subcontracted to a younger sister of the boss's wife, so it could be hard to improve. He suggested that we buy another factory's meal plan and eat there.
4. A wage increase of 100 to 200 yuan.
5. The production target ought to be calculated by workers' attendance. With a smaller number of workers working on the shop floor, the target has to be decreased.

6. We should get more gloves, which were not provided on the shop floor before.

7. The company cannot fire anyone who was involved in the strike.

He also said, in the end, that we could contact him directly if we had any questions, and he left his phone number with us. We thought this manager was nice, and we were so happy, like we had found a treasure. Everybody kept his number. In the beginning we were afraid that we wouldn't know what to say once he answered our calls, but people then found that the number didn't work.

Causing Other Lines to Strike, and Attitudes of Other Workers and Relatives

Workers in two other lines saw that our strike didn't have any bad outcomes, and management even tried to talk to us. They therefore thought that the company would only respond to a strike by paying more attention to those involved. These workers also wanted to skip work for a day, so they went on strike as well. Some nightshift folks went out and had fun with them and skipped their shift. Some people went out, some stayed in the dormitory and some on the shop floor. They just hung out for several hours and returned to work upon their supervisor's request. It was said that they would lose one day's payment, so they threatened to beat their supervisors. In the end, no wages were deducted.

People talked about the strike everywhere in the factory. When we went to get hot water, people would identify us by our line, "the line that went on a strike." When we went to other lines to help, we might be asked about the strike. People complained about the company after listening to our story. We were also invited to other people's dormitory rooms for storytelling—they were very curious and amazed by the strike. The conversation was usually focused, however, on grievances with the management rather than on the strike itself. People thought that our supervisors were just playing around all day but they got paid nicely, while we slaved away day after day for such low wages. People said that we should beat up the male supervisors, or they should lose their position;

they cursed the female supervisors that they should never find a husband. We mainly cursed supervisors but not the workshop manager. He was a high-level manager with lots of experience and a strong background, so we had nothing to do with him. We were just venting our anger anyway, but it's said that a supervisor did get beat up in another factory.

My cousin and aunt said that I was crazy. They thought I didn't do my job well. Some people have been here for a long time, they said, therefore we could tell the company was fine, and that we should work hard here.

Post-Strike Division among Workers and Personal Reflections

After the strike and before the next payday, people worked hard, with a high level of solidarity, as our wages had increased. After the next payday, we found that the wage increase was not the same for everybody, and conflicts began to emerge. I got a bigger increase than others, almost 300 yuan. Some people said that I might have sold out to management. When the workshop manager asked me whether I started the strike, I jokingly said, "I would not be working here if I were that influential." She said everybody said that I had instigated the strike. After the wage increase, three girls went to the office asking why I got so much. They didn't like me because I always went to work late, and during work I went to the restroom and drank water quite often. As a matter of fact, my wage increase was due to the fact that I had just gotten promoted to a higher rank. However, people openly showed that they didn't like me after this. I felt bad about this. Many good friends became distant all of a sudden. They even threw things in my face. It's just a couple dozen yuan difference between them and me; I think it just isn't worth it.

I think this strike was not very successful. It didn't last long, and the impact wasn't significant. We got a wage increase, but lost it again after three or four months. The company was supposed to raise our wage every few months, but they canceled this after the first post-strike raise to make up their "loss." And sometimes there's still an early morning shift.

The reason I quit was that the orders the company received were not as stable as before, and the wage was not high enough. I ended up finding another factory in the same town.

The Activists

The activists in this strike included: me, several other male workers, and some very eloquent big sisters. There's one in the packaging department and one in materials receiving. They had worked here longer, so people trusted them. Those big sisters were in their early forties, also with comparatively long experience in the factory. They usually worked slowly, and liked to criticize our line leader. They were quite humorous, so people liked them and were willing to hang out with them. We jokingly called them grandmas, because some of them even had kids older than we were. They took care of us a lot. Sometimes they gave us instant noodles and oranges during overtime. They brought the food to the shop floor secretly and put them under our workstations. Younger people were not that experienced and unfamiliar with this practice, so they often felt hungry. Although the big sisters weren't formally educated, they really knew how to talk. They were from Hubei, and they wrote us letters when they went back. The younger ones were not that active. They had huge financial burdens at home. Having left home since the age of thirteen or fourteen, some of them were the same age as me. They felt this factory was better than where they were before. The factories they used to be in were even worse, so they found this one relatively satisfactory.

Conclusion

I used to like working in big factories. Orders there were more stable, there's overtime every day, and the company paid regularly. People like this kind of place. Turnover was low, at most one or two people leaving every month.

It was an advantage that our dormitory wasn't managed and workers could switch rooms freely. During the strike we moved to rooms next to each other to ensure solidarity. Fearing that we might be caught, we hid in blankets when talking to the manager to protect our identities.

I didn't know too much before, so I was brave. Now I know more, but I'm afraid of more things, too.

"On strike"

Section Two: Strike Leaders

The thirty-year expansion in the coastal industrial belt was predominantly based on high-intensity labor with low wages and overtime. This was the same, regardless of conditions in the market. Workers' income was low and could easily decline. Although minimum wages have been adjusted upward for years, workers' total income often reverted to prior levels (through the cancellation of benefits or the intensification of work). That led to lots of friction between capital and labor. Meanwhile, in the past ten years,[1] quite a lot of jobs were on offer in the Pearl River Delta, so workers did not consider a dismissal or resignation as costly. Even low-level managers (especially the young ones) could sometimes accept the consequences of leaving their jobs. For strikes, this was a favorable factor.

In the Pearl River Delta, strikes are mostly initiated by workers and occasionally by low-level managers. The reason for taking the initiative is either the violation of collective interests or mere indignation over injustice. Since this book's space is limited, only a fraction of the actual initiators of strikes are dealt with here. The workers who initiate strikes often show these characteristics: they have been out working for quite a long time and have extensive social networks; they are rather skilled or at least are not considered stupid, and they are not a burden on their workmates; they are usually friendly and helpful people and easily win the trust of others; some of them belong to the technical staff that control key departments of production. These people are reflective thinkers, they rely on themselves, and in a generally unjust environ-

---

1. Editors' note: This refers to the period of labor shortage in the Pearl River Delta beginning in 2003.

ment they are willing to bravely step forward. In 2011, during a strike against wage arrears in a Hong Kong–invested electronics factory, a warehouse manager who frequently spread information on the defense of legal rights got together with a small number of colleagues. He cut the electricity, thereby bringing the whole factory to a halt. In 2005, a group of senior women workers played a prominent role during a strike in an electronics factory. They lacked a "good" education, but they had courage, dared to speak up, and cared about their colleagues.

Why would low-level managers start a strike? Unlike ordinary workers, low-level managers are partly relieved from productive labor (like line leaders, team leaders, or group leaders). They work the same hours, but their work is a bit more relaxed. Most line leaders enter the factory rather early, so some benefits linked to seniority disproportionately benefit managers (for instance, the year-end bonus). Since their situation is a bit better, if workers' income declines (for instance, through the reduction of overtime payments), conflicts with low-level leaders often become even more sensitive. More importantly, workers' resentments affect the line leaders directly, because they'll feel "pressure from above and heat from below." When low-level managers agitate for or order a stop to production, it usually indicates that the contradictions in the factory have reached a certain level.

After workers start a strike, maintaining communication and trust during the struggle poses a big problem. Sometimes the initiators complain that workers are not defending them. The warehouse manager who cut the electricity to stop production grew disillusioned when he saw the workers nearby just sitting there and watching him being "arrested" by the security guards. More often, workers expect the initiators [of a strike] will be bribed and defect to the enemy, easily believing rumors to that effect. In 2004, during a strike at a Hong Kong–invested battery factory, workers' representatives had been out to file a petition with the government. They returned to the factory only to discover that everyone had already surrendered because they thought that the representatives had taken money from the boss. The representatives were extremely frustrated.

At first glance, it seems line leaders are better at directing and co-ordinating actions than ordinary workers. Sometimes they accomplish better organizational results. In 2004, during the strike in another Hong Kong–invested battery factory, a recruitment manager from the group of line leaders greatly boosted the morale of the workers, who thought (the line leaders set up a strike) "in the same way they assign a work task." However, the overbearing conduct of line leaders is dependent on the passive obedience of workers, while the development of any strike demands the active engagement of workers. Related content in this book as well as other materials illustrate that no matter whether it is low-level managers or workers, after the outbreak of a strike, both have limited control over the process—and definitely no decisive authority. Workers and low-level managers usually lack experience leading strikes and are neither practically nor ideologically prepared. Even if some initiators have discussed the matter beforehand, they cannot communicate with enough people, and as soon as the action starts it is hard to avoid stirring up a hornet's nest. During a strike in a large electronics factory in Shenzhen in 2005, several low-level managers who posed as the initiators had many different plans. For instance, they proposed ensuring order during worker assemblies; however, after the signal to stop production was given, the excited workers stepped all over each other in the huge crowd. Frankly speaking, in the current stage of the strike movement it does not matter who the initiators are; usually one can only play things by ear.

Seen from the perspective of the workers, low-level managers joining or even starting strikes may help to win concrete struggles faster. However, that is all it is. Many workers mistakenly think that [low-level] managers or department leaders "have the respect of the company owners and are able to talk to them," and that that will bring about better results. The result of this is that they are not prepared to deal with the difficult and challenging aspects of the struggle. Countless events, some of which are detailed in this book, illustrate that these [ideas about cooperation with managers] are illusions and nonsense. Take one example in this book: in 2010, in a Hong Kong–invested factory for motorcycle parts, a department manager with a worker background had a reputation of enjoying the "deep trust of the factory owner." When he once led a strike against wage cuts, the workers maintained the illusion that he could act as a middleman vis-à-vis the boss. They did not think enough about strategies to continue the struggle. The boss had the final word: "I can make sure that you (pointing at the manager) spend the rest of your life in prison!" The workers were confused and saw no other way but to surrender.

In fact, the layer of management between workers and company owners is more prone to compromise and betrayal [even when they have a worker background]. These managers always receive ideological training to be loyal to the company owners and therefore unconsciously adopt the perspective of the owners when facing problems. They are more determined than workers to change the fate of the company: after all, it's difficult to climb the ladder to become a low-level leader, and if they switched to a different company they might have to start from the bottom. When initiating a strike, they usually lack the stamina to withstand open confrontations. When leading a strike, low-level managers show [two] important characteristics: they are clever in dealing with small problems, but they don't follow things through to the end. In 2009, during a strike in a transformer factory in Shenzhen, a team leader ordered a stoppage of production and honestly told the company owner from beginning to end, "I'm doing this all for your good, to eliminate the hidden problems in the management of production." That strike was successful in pushing through a number of improvements, but the main reason was not the team leader's efforts, but rather the company owner's fear that orders would be delayed. Are there exceptions among low-level managers who stand completely on the side of the workers? Surely there are, but not many.

How can workers lead strikes in a better way? By establishing a base of solidarity and active engagement; by neither rejecting nor easily trusting the participation and leadership of [low-level] managers; by choosing representatives among the workers from each department, section, work team, and so on; and by summarizing the workers' demands and exploring the means of struggle, and supporting and holding accountable the main leaders of the struggle, whether these are workers or low-level managers. Only in this way will workers have a chance to win more of their demands and avoid being duped.

Chapter Eight

A Female Worker's
Three Strike Experiences

Interview conducted May 21, 2010

Personal Background

Female worker A'ju was born in 1987. She grew up in a village in Guangxi Province and is a member of the Zhuang ethnic minority group. Before finishing middle school, and without telling her family, she followed her older brother to Guangdong Province to find work. She left because she did not want to continue going to school. She wanted to work and support herself and hoped she could earn money. When other young people from the village came back for the New Year celebrations in their new clothes she was envious, and the old people said, "When you go out to work you can earn money."

At the time, her older brother worked in a stationery factory and an older female cousin worked in a printing factory, both in Dongguan. In May 2005, her cousin arranged a job for her in a factory producing inductors. A'ju was just seventeen years old and was surprised to take part in a strike for the first time in her life after just three months of work.

The First Strike in an Inductor Factory

During her time in the inductor factory, A'ju never learned the name of the things she produced. Usually, workers would refer to them by the product number. Later she joined another factory as a low-level supervisor and handled all kinds of products. Only then did she learn that the things she had produced in the previous factory were called inductors. That inductor factory had 1,700 to 1,800 workers, and 300 to 400 of them were in her workshop. Every workshop had seven or eight production lines. Every line had a group leader overseeing at least twenty workers. At first, A'ju worked on a packaging line with more than forty other workers, but within a few months she learned how to do packaging, testing, soldering, and other jobs.

Antagonism and Daily Conflict on the Shop Floor

Since all of the workshop's seven to eight lines had a group leader, an assistant group leader, and even a deputy assistant leader, there were a considerable number of low-level managers. The task of the group leader was to write reports and to head the "three post-meal meetings" (daily meetings after breakfast, lunch, and dinner, when the group leader talked about the state of production, quality, work discipline, matters that needed attention, and so on). The main task of the assistant group leader was technical instruction of workers and disciplining disobedient workers. This way the group leaders had little to do, and there seemed to be more of them than necessary. Among the managers on the shop floor, it was usually the deputy supervisor who was in charge. She often stood in front of everyone and shouted at people. As the group leader, she liked to pick up defective products and deliberately give workers a hard time. A'ju said, "I think the deputy supervisor is awful, because she's too controlling." Workers often wrote curses against the deputy supervisor on the back of the toilet door.

Because the supervisor was not directly involved, he appeared relatively gentle. A'ju explained, "It was basically the supervisor playing the good cop and the deputy supervisor playing the bad cop." So did people feel the supervisor is better than the deputy supervisor? A'ju said she did not feel that way, because when the deputy scolded workers the main supervisor would intervene and mediate, but he did not really care about the workers. Some workers would argue with the low-level supervisors (from the group leader to the deputy) because they often picked out defective products and gave workers a hard time. Each workshop had to pick out 3,000 defective products every day. The supervisors would often stand by the workers and let them pick out defective products themselves; when the workers were unable to get it right, the supervisors would intervene and then reprimand the workers. Sometimes the factory owner or manager would also come down to the workshop and start gesticulating, shouting and screaming about the workers' mistakes. All in all, the managers "did nothing but attack the workers."

Some workers secretly engaged in all sorts of minor sabotage and troublemaking to express their dissatisfaction with the abuse of workers, the scolding, and the unreasonable organization of production. A'ju herself often did things like that. The male group leader on her production line often came running over when he had nothing to do, trying to lure her into a conversation by talking loudly about some TV drama she had never seen; this greatly irritated A'ju. During packaging, she would deliberately pass on defective products. Once, when the group leader was scolding her, without saying a word she pushed the whole head-high pile of products on the line onto the floor. The deputy supervisor came running over and screamed: "What is going on here?" A'ju did not say anything and continued to work, leaving the group leader and the deputy supervisor speechless. The group leader told her to stand by the wall as a warning. She stood there and rubbed her foot up and down the workshop wall, until there was a line of dirty footprints on the wall. As punishment, the group leader told her to clean the high windows, but she stepped on the windowsills and left a complete mess.

Sometimes A'ju threw intact products down the toilet, or even clogged the toilets on purpose. She said that she had never thought about complaining or confronting the boss, she just wanted to piss off the group leader. A'ju was relatively daring in expressing her dissatisfaction. She said that in six years of working away from home, she had not met anyone like herself. Why? She thought that most workers were cowards.

Regarding relations with the boss, she mentioned one thing: when workers were very tired working overtime at night, they would play music on a tape recorder. An old man came and told them to turn the volume down a little because people in the factory dormitory opposite the workshop were sleeping. The workers looked at him with his straw hat and slippers. He looked like an old sugar cane farmer from the South. Who was he? Why didn't he mind his own business? Only later did they learn he was the boss. He occasionally came into the workshop but did not control the workers, criticize, or even talk to them. But A'ju did not think that was a good thing either. Telling the story, she seemed very indifferent.

Wages

New workers receiving an hourly wage made 800 or 900 yuan per month. After mastering the skills they could make 1,100 or 1,200 yuan using a piece-rate system. Group leaders got significantly more than the workers; with an hourly wage, overtime payments, and commission, they made 2,300 to 2,400 yuan. The group leader could also decide whether the workers were paid an hourly wage or a piece rate. Some workers were relatives of supervisors (one of them was more than seventy years old), and those workers could get the better paid jobs, working eight hours a day and earning more than 2,000 yuan per month.

Workers' Relations

The workers had little time to interact socially. They had to get to the workshop before 8 a.m. in the morning and finished at 5 p.m. They had to work twenty-six days per month. Officially, weekend overtime was voluntary, but in reality, most Sundays, workers were forced to do overtime. Workers had no time to go out shopping or for dinner parties. Whenever they had time they would just sleep. A'ju herself was like that. Seven people lived in her dormitory room: she, one other worker, three security guards, and two of the security guards' relatives.

After one month of work, A'ju switched departments. A'ju had to cope with abuse and criticism from a low-level supervisor. After "bearing it for a month" she resigned. The deputy supervisor browbeat her for this, yet the supervisor continued to cajole her to stay (because she was rather skillful). A'ju told him: either you let me resign or you have to let me switch departments. As a result, she was transferred to the technical department and worked as a solderer. Forty to fifty people were working in the workshop. The job demanded a certain skill, and the workers had to go through special training before they could start. Wages were more or less equal, because there was a collective piece rate.

In the packaging department where she had worked before, most of the workers were relatively old (about forty); in the technical department most of the workers were seventeen or eighteen to twenty-somethings. When they were all together, they were often laughing and relatively happy. One month they worked especially hard, and according to the previous piece rates they should have gotten a wage of about 1,800 yuan. The deputy supervisor did not want "the workers' wage to be too high," so he lowered the piece rate. As a result, each worker got only about 1,200 yuan.

Resistance and Strike

One day after the technical department paid out wages, workers openly discussed how unreasonable the wage was. They demanded back payment. During one of the "three post-meal meetings" workers fought to be the first to confront the group leader with their demands. Work speed slowed down, and workers even left their posts to talk with others. The group leader was under pressure, so he went to talk to the deputy supervisor. The deputy supervisor agreed to pay more a few days later. At the time, everyone believed him and demanded that the back payment be made within one week.

After one week, there was not the slightest sign of the payment. One day, at 6 p.m., someone—it is not clear who—proposed to strike by refusing overtime that evening. (Afterward the boss tried to find out who proposed the strike, but for the workers that was irrelevant.) Everyone in the workshop agreed at once. The group leader was asked to invite everyone for a meal, and he agreed without hesitation. Since the group leader's wage was linked to the workers' wages, and since his girlfriend was among the workshop workers, he got on well with everyone. Several groups of workers went separately to eat and hang out (the soldering department had three floors). The group leader invited everyone out for a meal; a dozen workers from the first floor went with him and three other group leaders joined them. Others went to a skating rink to hang out there. Workers from the day and the night shift left, and no one stayed in the workshop or in the dormitory. Since they refused to do overtime that evening, in the morning the next day nobody was there for the day shift. "So they went on strike. [If they want to fire us, go] ahead and fire us." During the meal A'ju talked to two colleagues she knew well. They calculated that if the management turned on them, they would collectively quit. Those two colleagues may have talked to other workers about this, too.

When the main factory gate was opened the next day, the striking workers formed several rows in front and pressed for their demands. The supervisor railed angrily, "No working?! What does this department of yours want to do?" An eighteen-year-old female worker who had already handed in her resignation replied, "Give us back pay!" The supervisor asked the workers to choose on the spot: those who wanted to continue to work had to return to the shop floor, start the shift, and receive a fine of 100 yuan each; those who did not want to work should step to one side and would receive their wage and leave.

The young woman immediately stepped to the side—but when she turned her head she saw that she was the only one. All of the other workers returned to the shop floor. The young woman followed the crowd back inside. The workers started to quietly discuss the matter. The next event stunned the managers and supervisors. One worker took a cup from the workshop and left. Then all the workers who had returned to the workshop (including the four group leaders from the technical department who had participated in the dinner the evening before) one by one took a cup or other personal items from the workshop and left. Obviously, they all wanted to "step to one side," meaning they all wanted to resign. Although A'ju had only talked to two other female workers the evening before and did not know what other workers thought, their tacit agreement came as no surprise to her. She said that, in fact, many workers did not want to leave at first but after the boss threatened them with fines they thought it was pointless to stay. If the boss had not said so, maybe they would not have left. But why did the workers take the cups out of the workshop? A'ju explained, "We meant it in this way: I would not even leave a single hair here." In other words, they would not leave even the most worthless of things behind for management.

When the workers returned to the workshop they had to pass through other departments. A dozen workers in those departments had already expressed their desire to resign, so they followed the others out. Altogether more than fifty workers left. The manager said, "You're not working hard, and you want to quit. I just don't know what to do with you." The workers just laughed out loud. That afternoon they took their wages, rolled up their mattresses, and left.

Later A'ju and twelve or thirteen colleagues rented a flat together and looked for work. Some of the female workers spent several months' wages on clothes. They went out again, looking everywhere for work. More than ten male workers, however, received phone calls from the managers who asked them to go back to work. Their jobs demanded technical skills, and the managers could not find so many workers all of a sudden. When they went back to work they all got a wage bump, and after that strike the managers did not dare to arbitrarily lower the piece rate again.

Post-Strike Reflections

For A'ju the most important thing was solidarity. She thought that a significant factor during the strike was the young age of the workers, most of whom had no pressure from their families. They were not afraid of being unable to find another job. She had no intention of harming the boss economically; she only wanted to enrage the managers and solve her problem more quickly. For her, the strike was "good fun," and she "liked to strike."

The Second Strike as a Strike Leader in an Electronics Factory

In 2006, A'ju took part in her second strike. It happened just one month after she joined the factory. The K Electronics factory was located in

Dongguan and produced battery chargers for mobile phones. It was managed by five Chinese businessmen. One of them helped A'ju get the job. In the previous factory where the first strike had happened, A'ju had been a low-level supervisor. That boss knew that she had "lost her job" and offered her a job in his own factory where she served as a group leader in the production department. Twenty to thirty workers worked on the production line. A'ju's basic wage was 1,200 yuan plus overtime; her monthly income came to 2,100 yuan. The boss thought highly of her and let her stay in an air-conditioned dormitory room where she lived together with office staff and managers.

On her first day, seven workers were involved in an act of resistance. The incident happened like this: The factory collaborated with another factory nearby. On A'ju's first day, another line's group leader arranged for seven male workers on her line to go to the other factory. Officially, it was about "training," but, in fact, they were asked to work. The workers did not like that, and upon returning they protested and wanted to go on strike. A'ju remembered what the boss (who had offered her the job) said: You need to treat the workers a bit better, you need to learn to "cajole" them. So she asked the workers to help her keep face, that is, to not go on strike, and she promised to take them out for dinner that evening. That way the issue was settled. If those seven workers had gone on strike, the entire production line would have been unable to operate normally.

Relations between group leaders and workers were generally tense. The managers and group leaders often scolded the workers. If the workers did not address the group leader as "group leader" or "top dog" they could be harshly reprimanded. The workers believed the group leaders acted so rudely because they were all married, and some of them had close relationships with the bosses. A'ju treated workers comparatively much better. When she initially joined the factory, some workers called her "top dog," and this gave her "goosebumps all over." She told the workers they did not have to work that hard, since they got an hourly wage anyway.

The workers had several problems they were concerned about: the production target was set too high, the overtime hours were too long, and so on. One male worker had previously worked in the quality department as a QC (quality controller). The supervisor did not like his appearance and deliberately gave him a hard time; he even transferred him to the production department where he continued to make things hard for him. One night at midnight, the manager ran into the dormitory and ordered him to leave the factory immediately. The worker's best friend (one of the seven previously mentioned workers who had resisted) protected him. The manager called the security guards and kicked them both out.

When the morning assembly started the next day, A'ju realized that two people were missing. She asked the workers about it, and after learning what had happened the previous night she got really angry: "I never approved this decision. To not inform me in advance is to disrespect me." Besides, where had the workers stayed after being dismissed in the middle of the night? They could not have slept on the street, could they? She was irritated and angry, and she told the whole group at the production line: now I cannot arrange all the work posts. (If one post at the production line was unoccupied, work was interrupted and a replacement had to be found.) Everyone act accordingly; in one day we can produce just one product (normally several hundred parts were produced each day).

Thus the workers stopped working, and hung out and chatted all day, while the production line continued to run. A'ju sent out text messages and made phone calls to the male workers who had been fired and told them about the strike. She thought that the dismissals were unjust, and that made her angry, so she went on strike.

The supervisor came running quickly. He asked what was going on and who was leading the strike. Nobody said a word. At that moment, A'ju was under a lot of pressure, although she believed the workers would not reveal that she led the strike. Still, she was afraid that if it came out, she would not be able to get her wages. At that point, the boss who had offered her the job came round.

The manager said: Those who do not want to work should step to one side. A'ju stepped to the side. That boss immediately stepped forward to stop her, but she held her stance. Although the workers had not moved to the side, they one by one said they would not work. In the end, all the workers from the production line resigned together with A'ju and settled their wages.

The Third Strike with the Whole Workforce in Another Small Electronics Factory

The third strike happened in a different Dongguan mobile phone battery charger factory with more than one hundred employees. At the time, A'ju had lost her ID card and had no other option but to apply for a job as an ordinary production worker in a small factory. Unexpectedly, it was easy to get the job. She just had to fill in a form and was hired. A'ju's job was to test mobile phone battery chargers. Since she had work experience, she quickly mastered the job.

There were all kinds of big and small problems: wages were low, wage payments included counterfeit money, workers could not resign (A'ju had just entered the factory when she bumped into workers who had this problem), and the food was full of worms.

One day they had noodles for breakfast. Only after many people had already eaten it did they discover that it was full of worms. Since it was very dark in the canteen and the light was not switched on in the morning, the people who had eaten it did not notice, but later more careful workers took the noodles outside to check them. Workers jokingly told A'ju, "Hurry up and eat breakfast! There is an extra snack in the noodles!" She was curious and went over, but she did not find anything in the noodles—by then factory managers had already scooped the worms out. She used a spoon to get to the bottom of the noodles. She had a close look and discovered many small worms. When the workers went back to the workshop and started the shift there was a lot of talk about that incident and other problems in the factory.

During the lunch break the discussions continued and apparently some male workers started to talk about a strike. Many workers did not go back to work, and A'ju decided not to work either. Around 2:30

or 3:00 p.m., the supervisor of the production department went to the dormitory and asked the workers to return to work. Some colleagues ran around and invited everyone to assemble at the dormitory. A'ju went there with several coworkers she knew well. Ten to twenty female workers got together in the dormitory. Most of them did not know each other and started to shoot the breeze.

Apparently, people from every production line had come. The supervisor stood at the door and shouted that the workers should come outside. The workers did not pay attention and did not respond. Finally the supervisor proposed that they go over to the canteen to negotiate and solve the problems. Only then did they leave the dormitory and walk over to the canteen. Workers from throughout the factory came to the canteen. The supervisor asked them why they had gone on strike. The workers did not say anything. The supervisor decided to call out the names of the workers and force them to answer one by one. There were all kinds of "responses": "There is not enough to eat, so I have no strength to work"; "You have not paid the wages, how should we be in the mood to work"; "The food is no good"; "I resigned, but you won't let me go; why should I go to work?"

The result of the strike was that the food got better (more meat, better taste). Wage payments did not include counterfeit money as often. The wages were paid—as in the bigger factories nearby—on the fifteenth of the month, instead of on the twentieth. Two or three weeks later, A'ju resigned. She said that the most important problems of that strike were that a) the workers' demands were too minor, and b) the strike lacked preparation.

Various Attitudes of Strike Leaders and Participants

All three above-mentioned strikes occurred in electronics factories in Dongguan. They started for different reasons: deduction of wages, arbitrary attacks on workers by managers, and bad food. In all cases, workers involved in the strike left the company afterwards. A'ju herself was a strike leader in the second case (2006). In the first case (2004) and the third case (2007), she joined a strike others had started. A'ju had the following reflections on the difference in her mentality as strike leader versus participant:

1. As a strike leader she was very angry. When she just joined the strike she was having more fun and was happier. Especially during the first strike, when the group leader took them for a meal, she was very happy.

2. As a strike leader she was under more pressure. She was afraid the workers would reveal she was a strike leader and she would not get her wages. If she had just joined the strike, either everyone would get their wages or nobody would. Also, she felt ashamed in front of the boss who had offered her the job.

3. As a strike leader, she actually stepped to one side when the manager said, "Those who do not want to work should step to one side." Although other workers did not follow her, they all said they did not want to work, which made her feel a little guilty. She even advised workers right then and there not to resign because she did not want people to think that as a group leader she would make other workers quit. When she just joined the strike and later resigned she did not have the same feelings.

Survival Modes and Psychological Development in the Industrial Zone

In the six years since 2004, A'ju has continuously worked at various factories. Altogether she has worked for more than twenty companies. One reason for the large number of job changes was her curiosity as a young worker. Another reason was her hope of finding a factory with better conditions. She thought it was a question of luck whether she would find such a workplace.

After six years, she had hardly saved any money. During the interview, she mentioned that she only had 150 yuan left on her. She was preparing to live with her older male cousin for a while before heading out again. Young workers' views of consumption have changed a lot recently. They spend a lot of money. They often go out in groups to dance clubs, shopping, and eating out, and they quickly spend all of their meager wages.

Would you want to work hard to "rise in the ranks"? A'ju replied, "I am not strong enough to bear the pressure. Being a manager drives me crazy. My older brother also does not want me to move up the ranks further." In the plastic factory where she started to work afterwards, A'ju had one finger on her right hand severed. That changed her attitude. She did not want to look for another factory, and she did not want to return to one of the factories with slightly better conditions where she had worked before: "One should not go back to past experiences; if you do, you lose face." In the beginning, she just wanted to be able to support herself. Now she was desperate because after her work accident she was not even able to do that. She planned to return to the village to develop an animal breeding business. At home, her father was breeding cattle, pigs, and sheep. He also had fishponds, and he was waiting for her older brother to return to run the business.

Chapter Nine

Interview with a Worker on Strike in a Shenzhen Factory

Interview conducted May 16, 2010

Personal Background

Xiaobei is twenty-five years old. Raised in a village in Yunnan Province, he is a member of the Yi ethnic group. He did not finish lower middle school and instead worked on the farm. He wanted to leave the village to learn about the world, so he moved to a county town where he went to a technical school to study electronics. In 2004, after just two months of training, his school sent him for an "internship" to Shenzhen. In reality, he was working as an ordinary production worker. This is how his life in the factory started.

After six years of work, Xiaobei said he had settled down in a factory, and did not see any big changes ahead. However, in the long run he planned to go back to his home in Yunnan despite the poverty there. The government was now repairing the roads and developing transport networks and the tourism industry. So there were some prospects for further development. Large building sites were looking for unskilled construction workers for 80 yuan per day. In addition, the prices back home were relatively low, so it was good for entrepreneurs. He planned to return to set up a vegetable greenhouse. Plenty of land was uncultivated up and down the hills in his village, and nearby there was a lot of virgin forest and plenty of high-quality water sources. The most important crops in the region were rice, tea, and tobacco. His family had five or six *mu*[1] of land but did not plant anything. Xiaobei said he had not done farmwork for a long time, but he was still confident that he could learn and master it quickly. In his youth he had worked on the farm and fed the pigs.

In his leisure time, Xiaobei liked to sing songs, and during the years in Shenzhen he formed a small musical community among his workmates. For nearly two years he and other colleagues had produced some workers' songs and put recordings on the Internet. At the time, he was too busy with work in the factory, so he did not have much time to participate in those leisure activities.

The Situation in the Factory

The longest period Xiaobei had ever stayed in a single factory was three years. It was a privately owned Taiwanese factory, and he took part in collective action there. It produced all kinds of small low-frequency transformers for electrical machinery. Most of them were sold to India and countries in Southeast Asia, and some were sold on the domestic market. The factory was located in Huangtian, and it was one of three factories owned by the same boss. The other two were located in Jiangsu and Taiwan. All of the factories together had 5,000 to 6,000 employees, and Xiaobei's factory had about 1,500. Most workers were women born in the 1980s or 1990s. In the workshops, less than 10 percent were more than thirty or forty years old.

Xiaobei started as an ordinary production worker. Then he was a technician for two months before basically serving as a team leader for two years. Soon after the victorious strike he quit the job. Xiaobei's job was relatively relaxed, despite the order deadlines they had to meet and the pressure of high production targets. Every half an hour he went for an inspection tour and checked the problems in production. Usually, there was plenty of time to just hang out in the team

1. On mu is roughly 1/6 of an acre

leader office on one side of the workshop, so he could drink tea, read a newspaper, and chat.

Management in the Factory

From top to bottom, the boss came first. He chatted frequently with the managers, occasionally had personal conversations with workers, and was intimately familiar with the production situation. A banner with big letters in the factory read something like: "Employees are the company's wealth, so to cherish employees is to cherish the company's wealth." This was not just a slogan—the boss also expressed that he really valued the workers. For example, there was no suggestion box in the factory because the boss was directly in control; when he got an important complaint it was posted directly on the announcement board, and he promised to solve the problem. In addition, the name of the complainant was not revealed. And when the boss saw managers disciplining ordinary workers on the shop floor, he often said, "How dare you treat my employees like that?" He always had this phrase, "my employees," on his lips, and he emphasized to the managers: whatever happens, you should not scold the workers. From top to bottom there was a common understanding: Do not arbitrarily discipline people, or, at least, do not scold workers in front of everybody in the workshop. If there is a complaint, call the person into the office and explain it slowly.

Xiaobei said the boss had also moved up from being an intern and team leader, thus he really understood the importance of the ground level and thoroughly understood management strategy. He lectured management staff in detail on how to treat the 1980s generation, how to treat the 1990s generation. He also frequently held trainings for management staff, and he was so articulate that the latter would sometimes take notes and study them. The day before the holidays, he would invite all of the workers to go out to eat. That happened twice a year, and some people would get drunk.

The boss's assistant was the vice director, and next was the assistant director. After that came the factory manager and his deputy, and in the workshop there were the department leaders and the group leaders.

The factory had more than ten departments, including the engineering department, the production department, the purchasing department, and the financial department. The responsibilities were clearly defined, as was the division of labor. The production department was divided into two buildings (A and B), each with four floors. There was one workshop on each floor, and each workshop had eight production lines. Each production line had a team leader who patrolled the line and an assistant. Every team leader patrolled the line once every half hour. Xiaobei's production line had forty workers, and other lines had a similar number. The company used the 7S management model, adding "saving" (materials) to the usual 6S system, while some companies used 9S (further adding "efficiency" and "appearance").[2]

Xiaobei reckons that in terms of management strategies the company was far ahead of other Chinese firms. First, the responsibilities were clear. For example, whoever was in charge was actually in charge. It was not possible for a person of higher rank to intervene in the business of lower ranks. Also, Xiaobei discovered that the company's production department had more authority than in many other Chinese-invested factories: the production department had a mighty position in the company, sometimes displaying lots of attitude during work disputes with higher ranking managers in the company (for instance, by hanging up the phone). Xiaobei discovered that in many other companies the production department was weak and had no status. Secondly, when there was a problem in production, the problem was investigated first, then solutions were proposed, and only afterward were responsibilities checked. Workers would not be blamed first. Xiaobei took himself as an example. He penalized workers who had made the same mistake over and over again, but only after the workers had willingly and on their own initiative filled out the violation form. Thirdly, the workers viewed the management

---

2. Editors' note: 6S management builds upon 5S methodology, which was developed in Japan as a workplace organization method and was identified as one of the techniques that enabled just-in-time manufacturing. 5S refers to Sort, Systematic Arrangement, Shine, Standardize, and Sustain. 6S management adds "Safety" to the original 5S methodology.

style as rather relaxed. For instance, after two hours of work they had a ten-minute break. In the morning, they could do gymnastics with music, similar to the exercises in middle schools. Xiaobei still thought that compared to private Hong Kong or foreign companies, the ones owned by Taiwanese were a bit worse, but in comparison to the Chinese-owned firms they were much better.

Background of the Strike: An Overall Attack on Workers' Wages (January 2009)

In early January 2009, before the Chinese New Year, the company went through big changes.

1. Rest periods were often shifted, thereby reducing overtime payments. The specific situation was like this: the overtime payment for weekend work was 10.34 yuan per hour, higher than the normal overtime payment of 7.75 yuan per hour. In order to avoid paying the much higher overtime bonus for weekend work, management shifted the days off, compensating prior weekend overtime with breaks on slow normal workdays. All of this was caused by irregular orders and bad production planning. The result was that workers had to do shifts on Saturdays and Sundays but "officially and properly" only got the normal wage, with no overtime payment and instead got time off during two other days as compensation.

2. Control was tightened, and workers were penalized more often. The financial crisis that exploded at the end of 2008 had very little impact on that company. In 2009, the company did not get fewer orders, but rather got even more than before. Production was bustling, and there was more overtime work. The existing penalty system, far from being moderated, was instead applied even more strictly. Above all, when someone fell asleep during the day shift, this was noted as a small violation and led to a 100 yuan fine. Since they had to work long overtime hours, many workers fell asleep during the day, and were therefore penalized. This led to discontent among the workers.

3. Many benefits were abolished. For example, at the end of every year the staff of the entire company (including the workers) participated in a lottery. Many people got electronic appliances worth thousands of yuan or even more than ten thousand yuan, and everyone got at least the consolation prize of 200 yuan. There was also an annual bonus. After one year of work it was 1,000 yuan, after two years 2,000 yuan, after three years 3,000 yuan, and so on. And there was an organized trip by all of the more than 1,500 employees. One year they went rafting in Guangdong. They loaded onto a bunch of tourist buses, and it was a lively event. The company paid nearly all the expenses. There was also a place to read and relax and a dance hall that was often used for birthday parties. Any worker celebrating his or her birthday did not have to work overtime but still received overtime payment. These benefits and more were all abolished.

These changes were allegedly made because after the financial crisis started, the Taiwanese bosses in the area got together and all agreed to abolish such benefits. The workers obviously did not like it, but many thought there was nothing they could do because the benefits were something the company decided on. They were basically a boss's "gift," and they were not regulated by labor laws. So what could workers do about it when companies raised or abolished them?

Many workers used a form of quiet and passive resistance—they left. Before January 2009, the company's turnover rate was low; after the big changes, worker turnover increased immensely.

The Strike on October 25

The Situation before the Strike, General Discontent, and the Team Leaders

Xiaobei emphasized that before the strike occurred, all the workers were dissatisfied. That kind of feeling was clearly visible, but nobody dared to take the initiative. Xiaobei did not know much about what the workers were thinking because the living quarters of low-level supervisors and that of workers were separated. He only knew that on the low-level supervisors' side people had strong opinions. They often talked loudly in the office next to the workshop, even criticizing upper levels of the company. Besides, relations between low-level supervisors like team leaders and assistants with the workers were not as confrontational as in other factories. Xiaobei believed, "Team leaders and workers formed a single front."

The basic wages and overtime payments of team leaders and workers were the same. The difference lay in the fact that team leaders got an additional job allowance of 200 yuan, free accommodation and food, some cost-of-living benefits, and sometimes a "red envelope" (with extra payments). So Xiaobei's emphasis on the "equality" of team leaders and workers seems exaggerated: the total income of team leaders added up to 3,000 yuan, assistants got 2,100 to 2,200 yuan, and workers 1,500 to 1,800 yuan. So there was a big difference. However, the sentiments of team leaders and workers were indeed pretty close.

Xiaobei said that team leaders were recruited from inside the company. They were promoted from the workforce to become team leaders or assistants. Some team leaders claimed "team leaders make the biggest contribution and should get the highest wage in the company." The team leaders had good relations with each other, and if there was a common problem they all sat down together to discuss it.

Sometimes a team leader would scold a worker, but that was seen as a matter "concerning only the incident at hand," and after one hour it was forgotten. It did not happen as often as in other factories, and did not affect personal relationships or lead to antagonism with workers. Outside of work, team leaders and workers often went out for meals and they were on good terms. Xiaobei felt that many other team leaders had even better relations with workers than he. He said that the team leaders and assistants at the two or three production lines in the same workshop were all under his leadership—an advantage for the strike.

The Fuse: Senior Management Starts a Row in the Workshop

On the morning of October 25, 2009, just after work had started at 8:00 a.m., an assistant manager came down to the shop floor for an inspection tour. He discovered that a thirty-seven- or thirty-eight-year-old female worker was not using protective gear, so he took her ID card and ordered Xiaobei to make a note of her violation. Xiaobei did not approve of the punishment. First, he thought the company was responsible for providing protective gear. But instead it had reduced its investments in occupational health and safety, and they did not have enough protective gear to go around. This was why some workers did not use protective gear, so it was not the workers but the company that was to blame. Secondly, Xiaobei thought that even a high-level manager had no right to bypass other ranks and interfere with the business of the low-level management. To solve a problem, he should talk to the respective managers.

Xiaobei had an argument with the assistant manager straight away, and it got increasingly fierce. The assistant manager shouted at Xiaobei in the workshop. Xiaobei was not happy about that and did not like the assistant manager's tone. Also, he felt that being openly criticized in front of his own subordinates in the workshop made him lose face. While the assistant manager walked from one end of the line to the other and continued to denounce him loudly, Xiaobei retorted, "You are making trouble for no reason!" He continued to oppose any punishment for the female worker and insisted that when workers did not use protective gear the company managers were to blame for it.

Xiaobei believed that punishment only made sense if it convinced workers, and if workers knew why they were being punished. He thought to himself, "A newcomer like you, who still does not understand what is going on, and you dare to be this self-important!" In reality, Xiaobei had already worked there for three years, and he was considered to be one of the "old employees" in the company.

In the workshop, all the workers and team leaders heard how Xiaobei argued with the senior manager, but the workers said nothing and continued to work. The female worker who was about to be punished then started to sob quietly. Subsequently Xiaobei told her that this issue "was not about you, it was just something between us managers." While the assistant manager continued to complain and shout, Xiaobei suddenly screamed, "Stop!" and then went to shut down his production line. That was the moment when the forty workers on that line stopped working. The strike had begun.

The Beginning of the Strike

Xiaobei walked over to the other production lines and shouted: "Why are you still working? Stop the lines!" Immediately the other lines were switched off. All the workers stopped working, and they were excited because—exhausted from work—they were able to take a break. As a result, all the three hundred–plus workers in Xiaobei's workshop on the second floor of factory building A laid down their tools. When the assistant manager saw this, he quickly ran back to the office building.

At this point it was about 9 a.m., and the workers and team leaders from floor 2 immediately assembled. Xiaobei told everyone in the workshop: If we do not work, we will quickly solve the problem. Everyone should line up now and go down to the courtyard and assemble, and nobody should leave the area. He continued, by emphasizing that nobody should create disorder, "If people block the road, it is their own responsibility." Xiaobei explained and suggested to everyone, "If management comes to me and wants to negotiate, if they put pressure on me and demand that I tell everyone to return to work, nobody should listen to me." He wanted to guarantee that the problem would be resolved, and only then would the action be over. After he spoke, the workers lined up in an orderly manner and went downstairs.

Meanwhile, Xiaobei ran to the first, third, and fourth floors and called on everyone there to join the strike: "You are all tired, take a break!" "We are on strike on the second floor, you should also do something!" He asked everyone to assemble in the courtyard. When the workers from factory building B saw what was happening, they also joined the strike and came downstairs. Some lines had not stopped, and the goods piled up there. But a small portion of the workers hesitated and did not come downstairs. Most of those workers were in their thirties and forties, "old workers" with seniority, some of whom had worked there for six or seven years. There were ten to twenty such workers in each workshop. Those who rushed in front were the young workers, who were seventeen or eighteen years old, many of whom were interns from technical schools and came from far away (for instance, Hunan or Henan). Xiaobei noticed that some interns came from the "Hubei School for Business Administration," but there were also some with technical college diplomas. The "old workers" who stayed upstairs to wait and see only came down when the assistant manager came with a megaphone and started to address the assembly.

However, this is not to say that all "old workers" were conservative. Some of them were even more excited than the young workers. "As soon as they heard the word "strike," whoosh, they came running down the stairs."

Assembly of the Striking Workers in the Courtyard

The striking workers had assembled in the courtyard, including low-level supervisors (team leaders, their assistants, and so on), production workers, and even the workshop's janitorial staff. Everyone was very excited. Some were chatting, some were playing with their mobile phones, others were singing. Everyone took this sudden strike as a rare break from work and they were not concerned about possible wage deductions, because everyone had swiped their cards at the beginning of the shift. During the assembly the participating management staff formed their own group, as they did not want to scatter among the workers. This was because they hoped the company would not view them as the strike organizers. The strike continued into the afternoon. At lunchtime, some workers went to eat but returned afterward.

Not long after the strike started, the assistant manager came with a megaphone and shouted to the workers in the courtyard, "What do you want? Don't hesitate, just tell us!" Nobody paid attention to him. He shouted again, "What do you propose? Just speak out!" Nobody paid attention. Finally, the assistant manager shouted, "Who wants to work, please, raise your hand!" No reaction. "Who doesn't want to

to Xiaobei and asked him straight away, "How much damage have you caused the company by what you did?" Xiaobei answered:

1. Today's strike was largely caused by company management problems. It was not my fault.

2. The workers were generally dissatisfied. Today's incident was caused by a small problem that led to a widespread eruption of discontent. It was not me alone who created it.

3. Indeed, I take some responsibility for today's strike (despite being a low-level supervisor I played a role in the strike) but, for you, this actually brought some advantages. What kind of advantages? It made you realize that there were problems, and this will lead to an improvement of company management. The employment ads you have posted will attract more people; when the factory improves, you will also feel better.

When asked whether, looking at it from the perspective of the company and its interests, he would feel he had benefited, Xiaobei responded, "This way it is even clearer that leading this strike was not for individual interests. It was for company interests, with benefits for individual protection." After hearing such vehemence, the boss kept silent for a moment and then said, "Still, you should write a self-criticism." Xiaobei thought this boss was pretty good. If it were another boss, he simply would not listen and immediately send you packing.

Resignation and Xiaobei's Personal Motivation to Support the Strike

When Xiaobei talked to the boss he mentioned resignation. The boss asked, "What? You're thinking of resigning?! You have done all this. How will you make up for it?!" Apart from the question of whether he wanted to evade responsibility, Xiaobei thought that the boss also recognized his value. Before, when Xiaobei was a technician, he had designed and tested products for the boss and his job status had been quite high.

Xiaobei had thought about quitting earlier, but all his applications for resignation were refused. Despite this, he did not decide to go on strike because he wanted to resign. The application for resignation had more to do with his personal prospects for promotion. He thought that in a big factory (like the factory he was working for at the time) competition was fierce, and it was always hard to get promoted. In a small factory there would be fewer employees and less competition, so it was probably easier to get a promotion. In addition, he felt that staying in one factory for too long got boring and tedious, so he wanted a change of environment.

Regarding his personal motivation to go on strike, he had had no other thoughts and had not been influenced by any ulterior motives. There had been absolutely no plan. When he argued with the senior manager at the time, it was his anger that drove the situation.

Two days after the strike, on October 27, Xiaobei took just half the monthly wage for October and quickly resigned. Everyone knew that he had applied for resignation earlier, so when he quit the job after the strike it looked natural. There were no regrets, but he felt he had to change his environment to be able to develop further.

Experiences

After the strike experience, some front line workers were happy and said, "It would be good to do this kind of thing more often." Xiaobei told them, "It's not so simple. If you're striking every day, why did you come out to work? It would be better to pack up, quit, and go back home." The strike had somehow changed the mentality of the workers. Before, when many workers wanted to demand improvements from the company, they thought that it was totally impossible. People generally stayed passive. Xiaobei asked an employee once, "Weren't you always saying before this was not possible and that was not possible? Why is it all possible now?" That worker argued, "Because now we have a lot of people (working together)!"

Xiaobei summed up the strike as follows:

First, the strike was much more effective than arbitration or filing a lawsuit. The boss gets very nervous when you just stop working and nobody shows up for the shift. That way the problems get addressed quickly. It has a bigger impact, and brings better results. If you file for arbitration, you have to wait for several months, and it is very difficult to get problems resolved.

Secondly, if you want to organize a collective struggle, you need to get everyone's backing first (same unfavorable situation, same dissatisfaction). On that basis, even if only a minority of the coworkers start to act, it is possible to mobilize a larger group. For instance, twenty or fifty workers are able to mobilize more than a hundred workers for action.

The boss always pretends to be the good guy. He likes to talk about protecting workers when admonishing lower-level managers, particularly during the strike on October 25. According to Xiaobei, many workers were very happy and proud because of that, and even "looked upon the boss as a god." Xiaobei thought about that and said, "That is my random metaphor but, in fact, it's not that much of an exaggeration." But the workers will be happy about it for a few days; then they will wake up and realize the boss is saying one thing and doing another. He is only thinking about his own interests.

Triggering Strikes in Neighboring Factories

For workers in neighboring companies, the strike in Xiaobei's factory served as a model. Two days after the strike, another one occurred in one of the nearby factories. It was a Hong Kong–invested company, employing more than five hundred people that produced high-frequency transformers (used in sockets, boards, and so on). That factory's workshops and the workshops in Xiaobei's factory were very close, and administrative staff and production managers of both factories often exchanged information and even parts. Some female workers would prepare breakfast for male workers they knew in the other factory. So information was passed along very quickly between those two factories. Workers from the neighboring factory therefore learned about the strike quickly, and that led to many discussions. The wages in that factory were far lower, and normally the difference in weekend overtime payments was 7 to 9 yuan. Workers secretly circulated the message that they would organize a strike on October 27.

On the day the strike was to happen, the boss of that factory— without saying anything beforehand—invited the five hundred–plus employees into the factory canteen and brought in a large batch of Red Bull drinks, one can for each worker. After sitting down, the boss said, "Actually, I have already thought about giving you a wage raise." He continued and promised increased overtime payments and other improvements. Xiaobei said: In our factory we had to go through great troubles for one day in order to organize the strike; in their factory it just took two hours in which the workers did not even say a word, neither made suggestions nor put forward demands, and they were successful in reaching their goals. Afterward, the workers joked that the when the boss had said, "I had already thought about giving you a wage raise," there was something he left unsaid: "It's just that you had not gone on strike yet." To put it another way, "If we had gone on strike earlier, the boss would have raised our wages ages ago."

After the Resignation: Experiences and Impressions from Another Mass Incident

After his resignation, Xiaobei worked for half a year as an assistant for the traffic police on the streets of the same area (one of Shenzhen's numerous industrial towns). In April 2010, he moved to the industrial zone of another town and started working in a factory. For about ten days, he changed jobs five or six times. In some factories he worked two or three days, in some he left after only half a day. He thought that each one of the factories was shady. Now he had settled down in the quality control department of an electronics factory. Unfortunately, the wages were not as high as in that Taiwanese factory, but he still did not regret that he initiated the strike.

While Xiaobei was an assistant for the traffic police he also "experienced" a mass incident—when he acted as a "pseudo riot cop" and participated in a deterrence action to ensure stability. In December 2009, the D-Logistics company in Shenzhen went bankrupt, and it had not delivered goods to several hundred clients. Those clients (for the most part stall owners in a nearby computer shopping mall) went to the company and demanded payments. When the company rudely refused, the stall owners were furious and organized a demonstration. Among the demonstrators were many express delivery company employees who were waiting for their wage payments. According to media reports, the D-Logistics company had altogether more than a thousand employees in the Shenzhen area, and the wage arrears amounted to 4,860,000 yuan.

On the afternoon of January 21, 2010, those express delivery company employees surrounded their senior management who were already sitting in a police car, protected by the cops. Using a megaphone to shout slogans, the crowd chanted in rage, "Give us the wages!" Masses of people stood around and watched so that traffic was blocked for several hours. Then the police found a way to solve the situation by helping to register the clients who claimed their debts and by promising to provide support to settle the issue. Only then did the crowd disperse. Some days later, the Shenzhen city government promised to advance the money for the D-Logistics employees' wage payments.

Xiaobei said that more than a thousand people took part in that demonstration. The authorities sent several kinds of police forces to maintain order. Uninformed bystanders observing the troop formations would have found it quite frightening. But knowing the inside story, one would not know whether to laugh or cry. Those police forces were actually very complex and included law enforcement personnel from the Public Security Department, labor bureau staff, public security officers, traffic police, neighborhood police, patrolmen, security guards, district and neighborhood committee staff, and even traffic police assistants like Xiaobei. But many people wore uniforms with the "riot police" symbol on their chests and stars on their shoulders. Even the temporarily employed assistants like Xiaobei wore the same clothes, though Xiaobei still thought of himself as a worker. They had to somberly pretend to march in lines and stand together in neat "police force" formations, putting on airs.

Xiaobei said that the current attempts to maintain social stability largely relied on security personnel hired from other places. In some villages, for instance, the police force was actually made up of just four people: one police commander, one deputy, and two police officers. Many of Shenzhen's numerous "villages" are already extremely dense business areas, and around these "villages" are vast industrial zones and more towns. However, some villages have employed several dozen people from other places as security personnel, and maintaining law and order relied largely on them. Xiaobei told us a secret: if you looked carefully at the "fake police" stars on the shoulders it was not hard to see they were printed on the uniforms, but real police stars were pinned to the uniforms. Real police also wore hats with stars. From the uniform they wore you could tell whether they were real police or not.

Right when he started to work as a traffic police assistant, Xiaobei was asked to pay a deposit of 250 yuan. At first, the wage was enough to get by, with overtime, at 2,100 yuan per month plus food and accommodation. The job was to patrol up and down the streets. Controls were rather lax. Some workers would look for a place to sleep straight away after starting the patrol, since all you had to do was make it until the shift was over.

However, later the wage was drastically reduced because overtime was eliminated and the daily working hours stayed at eight hours. Monthly wages suddenly fell to 1,200 yuan. Those assistant employees who thought of themselves as workers obviously were not pleased, and when that mass incident happened the squad leader said right away, "If there is a real confrontation, we will immediately run!" While they stood in straight lines they were even "taking pleasure in others' misfortune," holding on to the hope: "This (mass demonstration) is very good. It should get even bigger, the bigger the better!" They stood there from the morning until 3 p.m. in the afternoon, and at the end of the shift they immediately left.

Xiaobei said that the current factory had only two hundred to three hundred workers. But he focused mostly on the future, as it seemed there were big prospects. They had recently set up several factory branches, so he reckoned it was a good choice to keep working for that company.

Some Further Comments

Xiaobei mentioned that he had read reports on the Internet about the suicides at Foxconn (within four months, nine workers had jumped off buildings to kill themselves). The media reports seemed to mostly report on the emotional stress, but Xiaobei himself thought there were all kinds of pressures: the pressure at work, of being "fucked" [people from Guangdong and Guangxi Provinces used this word for being *scolded*[4]], some emotional sensitivity, the emotional stress of romantic breakups, and more. He thought that many things printed in the newspapers were not true. He himself had experienced these things. When a journalist interviewed him, Xiaobei was asked to stand in line with other traffic police assistants. They then, one by one, responded to the journalist's questions according to regulations. The first time it did not sound right, so they were asked to perform another time and lined up again. But it was still not satisfactory. So they had to "perform" several times.

As someone of the 1980s generation, Xiaobei reckoned he was still able to bear hardships. The problem with the 1990s generation was that it is not able to bear hardship. The latter had rather unrealistic expectations concerning consumption and often called their families to ask for money. Even those who went out to work were asking their family for money—something Xiaobei did not understand at all.

Xiaobei also spoke of an interesting fact of factory life: many young female workers put on roller skates and wore a small backpack when they went to work. In the factory, they took off the roller skates, put on work shoes, and walked over to work on the lines.

According to Xiaobei, people in his hometown did not hold particular religious beliefs. One simple way of worshipping was to take some random animal's skull and offer it as a sacrifice. Today's young people did not believe in this anymore, but the older family members still did. Out of respect for the social customs in his hometown, Xiaobei still participated in these worshipping practices.

---

4. Translator's note: 屌, *diao*, literally: penis.

"I've wanted to give you a raise for a while, it's just that you hadn't gone on strike."

Chapter Ten

A Strike Resulting
from Increasing Labor Intensity

Interview conducted November 29, 2010

Factory I is a Hong Kong–invested company with thirty years of history. It has branches in Guangzhou, Shenzhen, and Dongguan with an annual revenue of more than 100 million yuan. The factory's main products are helmets and packaging for carbonated beverages, and it subcontracts for multiple global brands. Its products are sold in Europe, America, Australia, Japan, and Korea. The factory where the strike occurred was in an industrial area outside of Shenzhen, and it employed more than a thousand workers. The factory's wages were based on the local minimum wage, and after the probationary period was over, management began to pay social security for workers. Workers were paid every fifteenth of the month for the previous month's work.

The big boss was already more than eighty years old, and his younger son took care of operations at the factory—people called him "small boss." According to the workers, big boss also worked his way up from the lowest level, so he treated the workers relatively well. But since the small boss took over, even though the wages kept pace with the prevailing local wages, some of the benefits that workers once received started to gradually decline. Small boss didn't actually stay inside the factory. Instead, the day-to-day operations were overseen by Chinese managers, including a factory director, deputy factory director, manager, general affairs manager, production director, and so on. A year before, a new manager took over at this factory. Previously, when the factory director demanded increases in efficiency, the former manager would push back a little bit, but the new manager bought into the factory director's goal of increasing efficiency.

The Reason for the Strike

The workshop where the strike occurred had 117 workers. Other workshops had workers divided into two twelve-hour shifts, but this workshop had just one long day shift (with no night shift). This meant that during peak season workers did a lot of overtime, with wages topping 3,000 yuan. This workshop also had a relatively large number of workers with three to five years of experience. The manager of the workshop, Brother Zhong, came up through the ranks of ordinary workers and was personally mentored by the big boss. From the workers' perspective, Brother Zhong was able to advocate for workers' interests with management and he could also prevent fines, so he was highly respected among the workers.

This strike did not occur by chance. In fact, it was a long time in the making. The low wages and benefits, fines, and unending increases in work pressure led to a high level of discontent among the workers that eventually came to a head.

Increased production quotas

Even though the workers and management had signed a collective contract and wages were purportedly paid by the hour, in practice the pay system was a blend of an hourly rate and a piece rate. Apart from setting work hours—ten hours per day—management also set a production quota, and if the quota was not met during the workday, the worker was required to do unpaid overtime. Because of this method of calculating pay, the workshop manager would try to limit production as much as possible, while the workers needed to complete their required work. However, if they worked faster, it would lead to an increased production quota. Before Brother Zhong took his position as workshop manager he had the support of the big boss, so he was able to effectively protest increases in production quota. But when small boss took the helm, Brother Zhong's protests went unanswered. The workers reported that before January 2010 they were basically able to complete the required work within their shifts. In June 2010, management raised wages to 1,100 yuan according to the increased minimum wage in Shenzhen. But after this the production quota repeatedly increased. It was adjusted after July, which left all the workers feeling a lot of pressure, but they persevered. The workers then realized that because the minimum wage was higher in Shenzhen than in Dongguan, most of the easier work had been shifted to factories in Dongguan, while the more difficult work had mostly been shifted to factories in Shenzhen where labor intensity was greatly increased. At the same time, purchase orders had not been stable. In September, the production quota had unexpectedly been increased three consecutive times within half a month, and on the whole workers felt unable to complete the expected work within the allotted time. So they had to work unpaid overtime just to earn the same wages as they had before, and the workers couldn't take this. Under pressure from the workers, Brother Zhong went to management to negotiate a decrease in efficiency requirements.

Occupational injuries

The tools used in this workshop—like pliers and clippers—led to widespread injuries after prolonged use. Many people had deformed fingers, with some knuckles unable to bend or extend. While working, some female workers often needed to brace their bodies against the components, giving rise to damage to joints throughout their bodies. But there was no way to definitively link these injuries to industrial hazards. Some other workers had failing eyesight, and if they weren't careful they could easily cut themselves with knives. After an injury at work, workers were required to pay their own hospital bills, many waiting for years for reimbursement to come and often receiving no compensation. This type of work was not classified as especially hazardous, so there was no opportunity for special monetary allowances.

Benefits

Apart from production requirements, another reason that the workers went on strike was long-held frustration with management style. The factory only had punitive discipline—a tiny mistake could result in a 100 yuan fine—but there was no system of rewards and benefits. In 2007 the factory still had an allowance for working in high temperatures, but a year before the strike, the high temperature allowance was removed along with the night-shift premium. The price of a meal in the factory cafeteria had increased from the previous price of 3.5 yuan to 4 yuan, and every month 60 yuan was deducted from workers' pay for accommodations, even though it was common practice at many factories to provide free housing. The workers believed that this management system came down from the factory director and a few high-level managers, so this strike directly targeted those high-level personnel and demanded from the Hong Kong–based owners that the culpable managers be removed.

The fuse

Two days before the strike, a notice was circulated in the factory setting a new production quota, and if a worker was not able to meet it, he or she would not be given overtime. It was impossible for many workers to meet this new production quota and they could not put up with it. If using the new production requirements, many workers would not be able to work overtime and thus could not get the overtime pay that made up most of their wages. Or workers would need to work more strenuously to increase their speed while at the same time working unpaid overtime to meet the new production quota.

The Course of the Strike

On November 17, management had unilaterally raised the production quota again, so workers challenged this move in the workshop with a slowdown. On the eighteenth, all the workers walked out of the workshop together and assembled at the doorway of the management office.

At midday, the workers received a notice ordering them to the cafeteria to discuss problems related to production capacity with the factory director. However, when the workers arrived in the cafeteria, the factory director was not there, and there were just a few other high-level managers in his place. After that, a group of thugs entered and immediately began to push and intimidate the workers, threatening, "We will remember you guys, and if any of you dare to leave the factory gates, you will die." One female worker took a picture on her cell phone, and a thug knocked her phone to the ground, leaving a cut on her face. One pregnant worker was similarly roughed up. A team of local police showed up, and the factory managers immediately went over to "communicate" with them. Then the police chief's attitude shifted—he proclaimed that one hundred workers were all telling lies, and this couldn't possibly have happened. The high-level managers then pretended that they had no knowledge of what had just happened in the cafeteria.

After the incident, the workers' feelings of insecurity grew dramatically—they felt that their lives had been directly threatened because neither the factory nor society could guarantee their safety. They did not dare to exit the factory gates, nor were they comfortable staying in the dormitories, the cafeteria, the workshop, or any other confined spaces. They instead stood as a group just inside the factory gates to one side where there was open space and high foot traffic, along with the factory's security camera. Brother Zhong emerged as the leader who called the shots during the process—the work stoppage, followed by a blockade of the factory gates. The workers blocked vehicles from entering the factory gates, which led the Chinese management to call for the Hong Kong–based owner to come to the factory. Production in the other workshops at the factory continued as usual, but because one workshop in the middle had stopped working and vehicles transporting cargo could not enter the factory, the work stoppage in one workshop still had a serious impact on the production of the whole factory. Workers from other workshops helped out by bringing food and bedding to the strikers, and by evening more than one hundred workers slept in the bitter cold and wind of late autumn.

On the nineteenth, the small boss finally arrived at the factory. Workers from the striking workshop offered a signed petition with a list of demands. At the beginning of the document they presented seven itemized demands, including: a guarantee of workers' safety, an explanation from factory management for the fact that workers were beaten up, a promise that from this point forward management would not use a work stoppage as an excuse to sack workers or change job positions, the dismissal of current factory leadership, the provision of premiums for work under unusual circumstances, and guaranteed production purchase orders.

That afternoon, the small boss, accompanied by top management, the labor bureau officials and the police chief met with worker representatives and responded to the workers' demands. The police chief apologized for his negative attitude the day before, saying that the culprits had already been detained, but they could not hand over the culprits, and he said that the workers' blockade of the factory gates was against the law. Officials from the labor bureau said that the workers' demands had no legal standing, and that if the workers were interested in earning money, it was normal to get injured on the job.

The worker representatives were speechless with anger, allowing the small boss to say whatever he wanted. The workers were very dissatisfied with management's response since not one of their demands had been met. The workers were also a bit suspicious of the information they had received: First of all, they wondered whether their blockade of the factory gates was truly against the law as the police chief said. Secondly, they wondered if the law might actually support their demands for wage premiums and other compensation. According to management, the workers had violated the law, and if they could not reach an agreement that day, the next day the riot police would begin to make arrests.

On the eighteenth and nineteenth, the workers had already sent messages to multiple media outlets, but they had not received any responses. The night of the nineteenth, the workers contacted lawyer G and asked for his representation in talks with management. On the morning of the twentieth, lawyer G arrived at the factory. Workers ment was strong enough to "handle" the strikers. The local police chief and his subordinates went to the workers and arrogantly told them that their suppression is legal and they can shoulder the legal responsibility, but their strike is illegal, detrimental to national interests, and unpatriotic. After the suppression on the twenty-first, the twenty-second again brought more intense pressure. Workers were forced to compromise. In the end, close to a hundred workers chose to quit and they were forced by management to sign an application to quit their job, meaning they would only be compensated 500 yuan per year of service, in violation of the law. When workers were about to leave, management demonstrated insincere benevolence by offering a free last meal. Most workers took advantage, hoping to add more financial burden to the management.

"If you behave yourself, I'll just cut your hair. If you don't, I'll cut off your head!" (apron reads: striking worker; ax reads: ending employment; clippers read: fines; scissors read: repression)

the boss came, I would still refuse to dispatch the orders unless he fired me. So, for all these reasons, this was the time to act.

The dispatcher came and saw that I had stopped arranging and sending out the goods, and went back to inform the production lines. Then the factory managers came with a dozen or so security guards and surrounded me. Strangely enough, even before the security guards arrived the other warehouse workers had all rallied around me. But when the security guards barged in and trapped me in a corner, the others just stood there and watched. I was very disappointed. At this point, the production line workers had cut the power to their production lines and halted production. More than three thousand workers stopped work and even in just one hour would have caused great financial loss. Some workers had taken long sticks with them and gone to turn off the central electrical switch. Nobody then dared to turn it back on again for fear of being beaten. It was no more than twenty minutes after I had stopped dispatching the orders when the manager received a phone call to hurry over to the production line as an even bigger strike was under way over there. We all rushed over there too.

The workers had not put forward any definite demands. One said one thing, another said another. I put forward some demands myself. The first was about the nonpayment of wages for two months. The second was about the number of people quitting their jobs, and that they should be given permission to leave. The third was about the excessive work intensity, specifically that the time allotted was not enough to reach the output quotas. I demanded that the extra time needed to fulfill them should be counted as overtime. As soon as the strike began, the senior-level management of the company held a meeting and decided to give compensation to the workers.

The Settlement of the Strike and Counterattack by Capital

The strike lasted two days. On the afternoon of the first day we planned the strike. On the second day the company issued a bulletin agreeing to make up the wage arrears within two days. In addition, the workers who had already quit could contact management and get their back wages. Management used every method to try to intimidate me, saying that my refusal to send out the goods had seriously damaged the factory. Nevertheless, they were reasonably polite. The boss called me a "morale wrecker," a "terrorist," and "number-one enemy." He didn't fire me outright, fearing that I might cause more trouble. But before long he found several ways to make things difficult for me. Of course, if I had been the boss I wouldn't have wanted troublemakers here either. So after the strike was over I found that management had increased my workload. The boss said I had the ability to handle more work. When I first entered the factory I was doing the work of two people, and that was tiring enough. He said he wanted to cut back on the labor force, and so I ended up adding another person's workload. I could still handle it, although it was very exhausting.

The same afternoon some twenty strike leaders were fired. Their wages were paid out on the spot, and they had to leave immediately. It was strange that they didn't fire me, too. All those fired were ordinary production line workers. The dispatcher had played only a liaison role, and some had merely stood by and watched. The fundamental reason was an accumulation of grievances among workers.

Various Worker Behaviors during the Strike

The managerial staff did not join the strike because their wages were higher than those of ordinary workers. In general, they had moved up to managerial positions with some difficulty, so they were not likely to take a stand with the workers. The person in charge of the warehouse supported the strike initially until he saw the dozen security guards arrive—then he quickly abandoned us. When I was arrested by the security guards, he was the first to say that it was hopeless trying to stop me. But he was the first person the company fired. While others did not strongly support me, they didn't say anything against me. The office staff that had light duties also didn't join the strike. The strikers were mainly the production line workers.

The warehouse workers and dispatchers with whom I planned the strike were at first all filled with righteous indignation. But as things started to get serious, they started to back away. They thought that all they had to do was make a fuss and everybody would get what he was owed. They also worried about their positions in the factory for fear of being targeted by management. For all sorts of reasons, in the course of the strike those who were keen to look after their own interests became the majority. And so crazy people like myself came to the forefront, solving the problems that needed to be solved. I felt happy for having helped solve problems for many people.

The Motivation and Reason for the Success of the Strike

I worked at the factory for just over a month. From that very first day when I saw a pregnant woman worker brutally treated, I felt disgusted. When I was working in the warehouse I could sense the dissatisfaction of the dispatchers even though they dared not speak out. Some said that they needed someone to take the lead, and then they would follow. But there was no leader, so there was nothing they could do. It was the nonpayment of two months' wages that gave me the opportunity to take the lead and organize the strike.

Because I lived outside the factory compound I had few chances to socialize with my colleagues after work. We mostly communicated during work. If I concentrated, I could finish my work tasks in two or three hours. Then I would have time to discuss things with my colleagues. The most leisure time we had was during evening overtime. There was hardly anything to do for these two hours, so we would hold discussions.[2]

I learned about labor laws from scratch. I bought books to teach myself. Then I would explain the labor laws to my colleagues. We discussed problems of dismissal, lack of a contract, and what to do in case of nonpayment of wages. They discussed these problems heatedly. I

---

2. Editors' note: This story is lacking in some important details, as it is not at all clear why workers suddenly had much free time when quotas were so intense as mentioned earlier. Unfortunately, this is simply how it appears in the original.

was also able to put them through mock interviews and explain how
to look for a better job. Many of them were quite capable but not very
articulate. By making speeches they could help boost their confidence
and speaking ability. Often, one person would stand in front of seven or
eight people to practice. They were very diligent. So whenever we had
free time, my section was the liveliest. If any of the supervisors object-
ed, I would reply by saying that we were not hindering normal work.

Some Experiences

The experience of this strike was rather good. Cutting off production
was the most effective way to change things. Sitting down to talk with
management would never solve the problem. Going to court doesn't
work either. Only by cutting off the production chain would management panic and pay serious attention.

Laws speak more for the rich. Although I have heard of reasonably
just cases, the human factor comes strongly into play in the course of
legal rights protection. Some people know how to manipulate the law.
Now, for individual workers, they still need to rely on the law. But it is
better for a group to unite and then take the legal road or cut off production at their workplace. Going to the relevant government departments, they would say there is little they can do. Given China's current
system, it is better to cut off the boss's production.

Even the labor bureau people would advise us to go back and halt
production. If you halt production, you'll cut off the factory's earnings.
That will cause panic among management, and that way the problem
will be solved quicker. Previously we all thought that it was best to stop
the production lines. Now we feel that we should also coalesce into a
group and have recourse to the law at the same time because by first
going down the legal road we would be putting ourselves at a moral advantage. If the factory management decides to use its money to smash
our attempt to get justice, and after they've spent a lot of money, we
could then unite to halt the production lines.

Part III: Strikes
for Wage Increases

Workers going on strike for a wage increase do so obviously because their pay is low. However, this kind of strike has not necessarily taken place in factories with the worst working conditions. On the contrary, workers in many factories funded by investors from Hong Kong, Macau, Taiwan, and foreign countries with higher wages and profitability were more likely to organize and participate in strikes. Back in 1993, there were a series of strikes in foreign-invested companies in the city of Zhuhai. These strikes were started by the workers in a Canon subsidiary where the wages and benefits were among the highest in the area. Workers were dissatisfied with the limited wage increase (only 10 percent) announced by management. Based on the wage increase of local government officials and the inflation rate, they demanded a substantial wage increase of 30 to 50 percent. A strike was trigged when the capitalist rejected this demand, and workers eventually won a moderate wage increase. This struggle soon encouraged and inspired more than ten similar strikes in other foreign-owned companies. In March 2010, the Huadu Car Industrial Park in Guangzhou encountered a concentrated surge of strikes demanding wage hikes, followed by a similar tide of strikes in Japanese-owned factories in the city of Foshan. Anticipating imminent industrial actions, Toshiba and Panasonic subsidiaries preemptively increased wages in order to avoid more significant losses from strikes.

Compared to workers' defensive actions against wage and benefit cuts, strikes for higher pay are offensive. One clear example was the Nanhai Honda strike.[1] However, there is no absolute line between defensive and offensive responses. The implementation of the Minimum Wage Standards Act has played a rather important role in current worker struggles. An increasing number of firms have increased base pay while simultaneously cutting benefits in order to comply with the local minimum wage standard, resulting in hardly any increase in workers' real wages. This has increased workers' willingness to resist. Worker strikes at this moment are both defensive and offensive and are a protest against capital's resistance to government-led reform. The increasingly widespread knowledge of labor law along with increasing reports of labor disputes have significantly raised workers' consciousness. When workers were less aware, they usually complained about stagnant wages and increased costs of living. After they realized that their base pay was even lower than the local minimum wage or that their overtime compensation did not comply with the labor law, they felt much more confident and empowered to argue for their own interests: "We want what we deserve." The part of "what we deserve" here, of course, is not most or all of what their labor produced, but just their "legal rights and benefits."

By itself, the annual minimum wage increase is a very limited improvement, which by no means would offset the rising costs of living. It has become increasingly difficult for workers to support their families and even themselves, even if they work overtime. Many young workers and technical workers are quite dissatisfied with their inability to pursue a meaningful life outside of work (including dating) or new career prospects; this is because they have to depend on a clearly insufficient "minimum wage" and excessive overtime just to survive. Thus, it is not surprising to see a remarkable surge of strikes in China, especially in some highly profitable foreign-invested industries. The strikes that took place in 2010 in many Japanese auto factories in the Pearl River Delta exemplify this type of offensive wage demand. What needs to be noted

1. Editors' note: This refers to a widely publicized strike that took place at a Honda transmission plant in May 2010.

here is workers' lack of legal knowledge when they fought against their seemingly law-abiding employers. This actually encouraged workers to behave more aggressively and more on their own initiative. Workers frequently resorted to arguments such as "our income is not able to sustain life" and "it is unfair." During the 2010 Nanhai Honda strikes, workers demanded wage increases based, first, on a comparison between income and living expenditures; second, wage levels in the same industry; and third, wage differentials between Chinese and Japanese employees (more than 10,000 yuan). They demanded "equal pay for equal work."

For the boss, the lower the wages, the better—as long as normal production can be maintained. Some powerful capitalists might be willing to pay their workers a high wage to maintain productivity and stability. This is especially feasible for many foreign-funded enterprises in China, given the fact that China's relatively cheap labor brings them high profits and some space for potential pay increases. One problem, however, concerns the entire capitalist class. A unilateral attempt to raise wages higher than the average by a few employers is likely to irritate other employers who might react through the power of the chamber of commerce. Simlarly, it could disturb the efforts of the local governments to woo investment with cheap labor. From the perspective of higher levels of government, this might be viewed as detrimental to the overall development of domestic capital. Wage repression holds one additional advantage for the entire capitalist class when profit rates are not low: granting them more bargaining power to negotiate with workers who demand pay increases. The low wages of the Chinese working class have been decisive for the development of capitalism in China. However, accumulated discontent with low wages has provided fuel to the fire of labor struggles. It will grow ever bigger, especially during an economic crisis and high inflation. We need to understand this phenomenon better and make more effort to help with the struggle for pay increases.

The current worker struggle in China is not yet at a high level of development, as reflected by the lack of clear awareness of the fundamental antagonism between capital and labor as well as the shortcomings of some strategies of resistance. Readers may get this sense from the cases included in this book. However, the suddenness, increasing scale, and scope of strikes, along with rising frequency have already posed a looming threat to the capitalist ruling structure. While labor repression is still widely seen, it has become increasingly indispensable for the ruling class to discipline, pacify, restrict, and contain this struggle. The spokesmen of private capital have tended to appease workers, in order to incorporate them as their political bargaining chips. Some top-down approaches such as the 2008 Labor Contract Law and the 2010 Social Insurance Act reflected the ruling class's desire for reforms. These laws do damage to the interests of a few capitalists, but serve to sustain the stability of the exploitative order. When overproduction and resource constraints become normal for the Chinese economy, some small and medium-sized companies that are unable to upgrade have to withdraw investment and even exit the market, which actually benefits the rest of their competitors. In addition, there are always legal loopholes left for capital, such as using dispatched labor[2] to reduce costs. It is worth mentioning here that the number of dispatched workers more than doubled from 2008 to 2010. The distinct conditions, concerns, and struggles of these workers should also receive our attention.

One of the key approaches to reining in labor struggles is to reconcile capital-labor conflict through an "intermediary," which could be a government department, an expert, a lawyer, a journalist, or a human rights organization to engage in negotiation under "neutral" or even "pro-labor" auspices. The Zhuhai city government was aware of this approach as early as 1993, following a series of strikes in foreign-funded factories. Recently, governments have taken efforts to urge official unions to engage in rights protection and become a qualified intermediary. To some extent, these attempts have been successful. For instance, many cities are currently promoting a union-led collective wage bargaining system, which intends to rely on the government to change the previous (negative) image of the official unions.

---

2. Editors' note: "Dispatched" labor is a type of labor subcontracting common in China.

The following three cases of strikes for wage increases are far from enough to fully capture the struggle in reality, and are not representative. Therefore, our discussion on this topic will not be confined to these cases.

Chapter Thirteen

A Collective Slowdown in a Molding Factory

Interview conducted November 23, 2009

We were fortunate to meet and interview four workers in this molding factory, all from Guangdong and Guangxi Provinces. The one who talked to us most is called Xiaochun, from Guangxi. He has worked in this factory since 2004 and was promoted as a master worker (*shifu*) in 2006. His[1] sister joined him in the same factory in 2010 and now works as a clerk. One of the other girls [who joined our conversation] has also been a clerk in this factory since 2005. And the final colleague is an apprentice worker who came in 2009. The two girls[2] both graduated from vocational schools with the same major. This strike is relatively special since everyone—including master workers, apprentice workers, and cleaners as well as clerks—participated (except for the three bosses from Hong Kong).

The Factory Profile

The factory, hereafter referred to as X Factory, is a molding plant. It has only twenty-five employees, with no professional management. Master workers arrange tasks for apprentice workers and general workers. The

1. Editors' note: Here in the original text Xiaochun is referred to using the feminine pronoun, whereas in several other places in the text it is masculine. For the sake of consistency, we have translated it as "he."
2. Editors' note: It's not clear in the original which two girls this refers to.

factory actually serves as a workshop for another large plant in the area, since it produces molds with brands made there. The factory itself has independent production, administration, and financial accounts' and has not yet registered with the local industrial and commercial bureau. Since the three bosses from Hong Kong do not speak Mandarin, they only hire people who speak Cantonese. This is why all the employees are from either Guangdong or Guangxi Province.

Workers do not sign contracts with the factory until they work there for a few months. The monthly salary for master workers was 3,000 yuan (around $460) before the strike, while the apprentice workers only received 10 yuan (around $1.5) per day as the base pay, much lower than the local minimum wage standard. None of the workers have the so-called three insurances, namely, pension, medical insurance, and unemployment insurance. The factory provided acceptable dormitories but no canteens, so workers had to go out for food. Those whose families were local could go home for meals. The factory rarely had industrial injuries, but didn't pay enough compensation when they did occur. Employees are typically young, with all master workers born in the 1980s. Master workers are the only skilled workers in the factory, apprentice workers can be promoted depending on their individual abilities and independence in production. The daily work is organized by each master worker with their apprentices, and it is easy for them to cooperate. Some workers graduated from vocational schools, while others came with no experience. Clerks had to deal with daily routines such as answering phone calls, as well as handling the computerized molding design.

Strikes in the Main Plant

The mold factory is associated with a larger plant with thousands of workers. The majority of line workers there are middle-aged, while younger ones are technical workers. The factory owner once attempted to relocate the entire plant elsewhere. However, workers managed to go on strike, repeatedly blocked the plant gate, and once even blocked the road when they found the boss trying to move machinery at night. The

goal of the strike was to force the boss to retroactively pay their overtime wages as stipulated by law. The boss eventually paid the compensation in installments, but workers were still not satisfied and continued
to strike, since the compensation was still lower than the legal standard.
The whole process lasted almost one year from the initial struggle for
compensation to an achieved compromise, during which most managers stayed neutral while a few also participated in the struggle. It was
said that their wage and benefits did not reach the standard level either.

The Struggle in X Factory

Half a year after the struggle in the main plant, workers successfully received their compensation one after the other. Upon receiving this news,
a few master workers in late July 2009 discussed demanding overtime
remuneration, economic compensation, and double wages for workers
who had not renewed their contracts since April.[3] During the time of
discussion, many workers heard of this idea and apprentice workers and
clerks also expressed their support. But since they had no idea what
ought to be done, they decided to follow the activists. Master workers
had received a monthly salary, but no overtime remuneration or social
insurance payment. They were in a relatively better position, but still they
hoped wages and benefits could be provided "according to the labor law."
Most people still felt hesitant about taking action and wanted to wait
and see what would happen. But when two-thirds of workers became
aware of this issue, seven activists (the majority of whom were also key
technicians in the factory) went to the bosses to "casually bring up" this
issue and handed them a hard copy of an application for compensation.
The bosses felt embarrassed, and didn't reveal their position. Worker representatives continued to talk to the bosses every day, but they either
immediately changed the topic, blamed workers for this "unreasonable"
quarrel, or tried to reason with the workers. Whenever this happened,
workers turned around and ignored them. Their perfunctory attitudes
obviously disappointed workers.

---

3. Editors' note: There is a stipulation in the Labor Contract Law that employees
are entitled to double wages for all of the months working without a labor contract.

On the morning of July 23, some employees stopped working. In the afternoon, everyone stopped. The bosses insisted that they would not pay double wages to workers who had not signed labor contracts, and they would only pay overtime compensation for two years based on a very ambiguous calculation method. To put it simply, they were just stalling for time. They also asked for representatives from workers instead of talking to everyone. The bosses were discussing amongst themselves in the office all day, while workers were also discussing on the shop floor. There was no communication between them. Workers decided to go to the local labor bureau as long as the bosses refused concessions. The next day, July 24, one of the boss's friends attempted to persuade workers by saying, "Chinese should not fight against Chinese; let us sit down and discuss." The man paid close attention to the attitudes of workers, and proposed to have separate conversations with different groups or individuals. After encountering only anger from the workers, the man left awkwardly.

On July 25, workers added one more demand of "returning the deposits withheld from apprentice workers" to their list. The workers had reached consensus. At that time, the bosses put up a notice saying that industry sabotage would be regarded as absenteeism and employees who were absent for three days would be "fired without compensation." Feeling irritated and unreasonably treated, workers gathered that night determined to learn more about the law, and to investigate whether strikes are legal and whether strikers would face legal repercussions.

During this period, workers discussed the strike in dorms or on shop floors in the daytime and looked into documents about labor legislation and judicial procedures. They also contacted and consulted related organizations and government departments. They originally planned to negotiate privately with the bosses and only go to the local labor bureau when the private attempts failed. But with continuous concessions from workers, the bosses still refused to compromise and both parties became increasingly impatient with the negotiation. Most activists wanted to stay on strike until they won, but they did not consider what to do if the strike did not fulfill their goal. The rest of workers, while doubtful about the success of the strike, still participated in every discussion. However, a majority of the workers, including the activists, felt somewhat lost in legal reading, consultation, and discussion, and were unsure what ought to be the next step.

When all the workers agreed to participate in the struggle for compensation, they held meetings before each collective action. The issues brought up in the meeting included certain conditions to concede and whether they should go on strike. The idea of striking, according to Xiaochun's understanding, was not only drawn from the demonstration effect of the strike in the main plant but also inspired by media reports of other strikes. At the beginning, some workers did not support the idea. But when they started to learn the relevant labor laws, they became confident and more willing to join the others. Workers documented all collective expenditures during the strike, such as meals, water, printing fees, and agreed to share the expenses when the strike succeeded.

On July 26, workers decided to resume work from the next day (the twenty-seventh), in order to show their sincerity for negotiation. But they also wanted to let the bosses know that their resumption of work did not signal a concession. Once negotiation failed, they would go to the local labor bureau to complain. To their surprise, they were infuriated by the bosses' reactions to their resumption of work. The bosses had learned that the workers had removed their employment documentation from the offices, so they then threatened to call the police if the workers did not return the materials within ten minutes.[4] Feeling nervous and uncertain if they really did "break the law," the workers had to hand back the employment documentation. But they became more angry and determined to complain to the local labor bureau.

At this point, the bosses asked the security guards to shut the gate and let no one out. Some workers stated that this lock-in was actually an unlawful imprisonment. So the bosses decided to open the gate and the employees marched to the labor bureau. The latter called two of the

---

4. Editors' note: The workers needed these documents in order to file a grievance with the labor bureau. The implication is that the boss was suggesting that it was illegal for them to remove these documents.

bosses and asked them to negotiate with workers. One of the officials from the labor bureau treated workers in a terrible manner, shouting at them, "If the factory was doing things illegally, then why did you work there?" When it approached closing time, the officials there urged workers to leave. The bosses also asked the workers to go back to the factory for negotiations at 7:30 p.m.

That night, the bosses divided workers into three groups, one group of master workers with a daily salary higher than 100 yuan ($15.40), one group of master workers and clerks with mid-level wages, and another group of apprentice workers. Their calculation method was very ambiguous. The bosses insisted on paying only 70 percent of the wage as economic compensation, but later increased their offer to 80 percent. Workers demanded 95 percent, but later dropped the demand to 85 percent. But the two parties could not reach an agreement and workers left one after another. All apprentice workers were promised retrospective compensation for receiving wages below the minimum wage level, and therefore they signed the agreement.

The next day, eleven workers who did not agree with the bosses went to the labor bureau again. The labor inspection team asked them to choose three representatives to negotiate. Some managers in the local village committee also intervened to mediate the dispute. The negotiation continued until noon. All but one or two workers refused to return to work in the afternoon. The apprentice workers regretted signing the agreement. Workers wrote an arbitration statement and prepared to resort to the district labor bureau.[5]

On July 29, all employees stopped work. The bosses again brought a friend who had a factory in Dongguan and had dealt with strikes to help mediate the dispute. He suggested first calculating the total amount of wages based on the standard wage rate stipulated in the Labor Law before resuming negotiations. On the thirtieth, the wage (without the double wage) calculated by workers already amounted to more than 500,000 yuan. The bosses proposed to pay 70 percent of the

---

5. Editors' note: The district is the next higher level in the administrative hierarchy.

wages as economic compensation to master workers in four monthly installments. Master workers refused. The bosses also proposed to pay 70 percent of wages to the group that earned a mid-level wage, and full payment for the apprentice workers.

The Result of the Struggle

After repeated strikes and several rounds of negotiations, the bosses agreed to the following compensation:

1. Based on the daily wage standard, retrospectively make up overtime payment as well as 25 percent of the remuneration as economic compensation;

2. Based on the above standard (basic wage + overtime remuneration, average wage in the past twelve months), retrospectively pay one month of economic compensation for each year and also pay a seniority bonus;

3. Retrospectively compensate for the gap with the minimum wage rate and overtime remuneration, and pay 25 percent in economic compensation to apprentice workers;

4. Register the factory, sign labor contracts according to the labor law, pay social insurance, and redefine the one-month probation period.

The bosses had to pay in installments, since they could not pay this large amount immediately. The four workers who were about to leave the factory at the end of August would get all their compensation before leaving. The turnover rate of this factory before the strike was low, but after the strike, many workers chose to quit. For instance, three of the four activists decided to resign. During the course of the strike, workers changed their attitudes toward labor law from "being merely aware of its existence" to "willing to gain a deeper understanding." Later on, even one employee from the main plant approached workers in X Factory in the hope of organizing "a joint second strike." But since the labor dispute of X Factory was settled, they had to give this up.

Xiaochun told us that he had not been concerned with the possibility that the bosses would suddenly fire them all and recruit others because he felt no one would be willing to join a factory that was on strike. He also thought that if police had intervened and arrested them, workers would have become increasingly angry and would unite to take more radical action. But he emphasized the indispensability of collective discussions for any action that would help participants feel confident and empowered rather than pessimistic. During the strikes, some workers were worried about the possibility of it dragging on. According to Xiaochun, this was because of their economic difficulties due to the lack of savings, concern for their families, and the high cost of living. But since the strike did not end up lasting long and workers all punched their attendance cards even while on strike, the company continued to pay them during the strike. Along with the good compensation they eventually won, they felt relatively content with the strike.

In this strike, workers actually did not demand wage increases and achieved nothing in this respect. Xiaochun was still unsatisfied with the wage rate for master workers, as he felt it was lower than the average in this industry. But he did not think it would be effective to struggle for wage increases by going on strike for three reasons. First, there are too many people in China, which means the bosses can easily replace the strikers. Second, every year a large number of young people graduate from vocational schools and they are not experienced enough to be able to demand a high wage, which imposes downward pressure on the wage level of all skilled workers. Third, skilled workers do not have a standard wage level like the one for general workers, so they have no legal precedent to demand wage increases. If they are unsatisfied with their current employment, they can only quit and look for a better job. Xiaochun mentioned that after adding overtime, the wages earned by many general workers already approached those of skilled workers. He complained that compared to other countries, China attached too little importance to skilled workers.

Some Reflections

Given the attitude of the labor bureau, Xiaochun came away from the strike feeling that the government was very corrupt and had no credibility. He did not believe the official slogans such as "harmonious society" and did not believe the status quo could be maintained. When talking about workers from the main plant blocking roads, Xiaochun thought that it could be regarded as unlawful. But the action was specifically to attract necessary attention from the government—and workers had no other alternative, since "the government only paid attention to large factories and small 'annoying' factories." He told us that his willingness to lead resistance in other factories would depend on the unity of the workers. Xiaochun expressed that he would be willing to lead the charge if he encountered similar problems in other factories, but only if workers were unified. He believed that in the case of large factories with many employees, it was necessary to have leadership among workers in order to motivate and inform others, which is why he felt that someone needed to play a leadership role in the strike at the main plant. Xiaochun also told us that it was necessary to have some regular mediating institutions such as labor unions to help individual workers solve problems.

From what Xiaochun mentioned, we attribute the success of this strike to three factors: the bosses' fear of having delays in their orders, the government's fear of an uncontrollable escalation of the strike, and the main plant's desire to avoid being trapped in more labor unrest while still dealing with its own strike. With regard to the internal causes, Xiaochun said, "It depends on government, but mainly it relies on workers' own strength."

Xiaochun told us that workers usually spent time on the Internet or window shopping when they were off work. Sometimes, they discussed political topics when reading the news. Xiaochun viewed these discussions as an important source of knowledge, since he felt workers should communicate with each other. For example, one worker had collected many materials from some NGOs. As for his future plans, Xiaochun said he initially had no idea. But after working for a while, he gradually formed "some plans for the future." Before, he was reluctant to leave his hometown for work, feeling unwilling to compete with others. But now he felt reluctant to return home. However, he still said he would go back if he found nothing to do in the city and became desperate. He used to send money home, but has since stopped. This is partly because of the high cost of living in the city and partly because his family does not need the money.

Xiaochun realized that it was very difficult to save money in Shenzhen, since wages were too low while the cost of living was too high. He complained that migrant workers worked so hard for the city, but were still required to pay extra in order to send their children to local schools. He also complained that in Shenzhen the civil service jobs were only given to native residents and this kind of "monopoly" would only "enrich the haves but impoverish the have-nots," though the migrant workers contributed a lot to the development of the city. In the end, he said, "The ones who indeed drive the society forward are skilled workers."

Chapter Fourteen

Strike in a Large Electronics (Motor) Factory in 2007

Interview conducted October 18, 2010

Reasons for the Strike

The company promised to raise the basic wage before July, but even when the wages for August were paid in September, it became clear that the company had not fulfilled its promise. This might be related to the fact that the local government did not adjust the minimum wage standard that year. One more thing fueling the anger of production line workers was that the company raised the base pay by 50 yuan for non-production-line workers (quality inspectors, clerks, skilled workers, and so on) in August and even compensated them retrospectively with the pay gap for July. The production line workers who had been waiting for the government adjustment of the minimum wage became infuriated. On the night of September 12, night-shift workers went on strike. One other detail our interviewees did not know or simply forgot: On September 12, the first night of the strike, workers blocked the No. 107 National Highway for two hours and eventually were driven forcibly back to the factory by police in army uniforms.

On September 13, workers went to the national highway again. Around one or two hundred workers started to walk toward the highway, but they encountered up to one hundred community security guards with shields and truncheons. They formed a human wall and used their truncheons and shields to drive the workers from the highway step by step. Workers seemed to deliberately play cat and mouse with them, suddenly crossing the highway and running off in the other direction, which scared the security guards and policemen and threw them into disarray. They hurried to cross the road and used the same method to force workers to retreat. The police cars from Bao'an District constantly patrolled the area, talking through the loudspeaker and saying things like, "Workers in L Factory, your demand for an 800 yuan wage hike was already agreed to by the company [actually they only agreed to 750 yuan]. Please immediately disband. Otherwise, we will take actions to rectify the chaos according to the People's Republic of China Law on Marches and Demonstrations." The standoff continued until after 7 o'clock at night. After the police chased workers down one street after the next, the workers were eventually dispersed.

One Interviewee's Experience

I left my hometown for work immediately after graduating from middle school in 2006. My parents did not keep me in school because they thought it was unnecessary for girls to study much. Our village had only three graduates from junior high school that year. Girls in the village usually left to work after junior high school. That is why I did not take the entrance exam for senior high school when I was about to graduate. I had actually never thought about going to work then, because my parents used to encourage me to study hard and never implied or suggested that I look for work outside the village. Therefore, I was very shocked when they asked me to look for work when I was about to graduate. My father was very autocratic at home and no one could change his decisions. I was still young then and not yet very sensible, and I always tried to meet my parents' demands as much as possible. I had no ideal image of working away from home. Every time my elder sister came back to the village, my father always prepared good meals for her since he said it must be difficult for her to work outside and the food in the canteens must have no nutritious value. From then on, I knew that working away from home would be very tiring. I was born in 1990 as the third child in my family. I have two elder sisters and one little brother. At that time, my eldest sister worked in a factory (hereafter referred to as L Factory) and had not been home for one year. She came back home and took me out to start working. When I first went, I was too young to be hired, so I had to work in a less regulated factory as a quality inspector.[1] After turning seventeen in the beginning of 2007, I was introduced by my eldest sister to L Factory. We worked on different floors of the same department.

The Basic Situation in the Factory and Employee Relationships

L Factory was founded in 1959 and moved to Shenzhen in 1982. It produces various motors used in automobile accessories, household electronic appliances, electronic tools, personal care products, and other multimedia/audiovisual products. The factory employed twenty thousand workers in 2007, and at present employs thirty thousand.

The factory has high turnover, which imposed high costs on the personnel department. But there is not much that can be done about it. However, some workers have been working here for seven to eight years, some even for more than ten years. Job stress mainly comes from the production quotas. Since I am adaptable and can get along with others easily, my work position has not changed. Sometimes, my team foreman asks me to help with different tasks.

One team typically has twenty to thirty workers. We initially had a good relationship with management. The previous team forewoman treated me well since I was young and obedient. She often arranged more overtime work for me. Whether we employees can have overtime work or not all depends on the foreperson. Later we had a new forewoman, but our relationship with her was not as good as with the previous one.

I have a good relationship with my workmates on the production line. I was so young when I first started working that my workmates

---

1. Editors' note: The implication here is that a less well-regulated factory would be willing to employ child labor.

took good care of me. I also have many friends from my hometown in this factory. Most workers here are from Hubei and Henan Provinces. We chat a lot, almost nonstop, during work, about all kinds of topics, including gossip, personal experiences, feelings, entertainment, and so on. As long as the production is not disturbed or there is no hidden danger, the forewoman doesn't stop us from chatting. I used to enjoy hiking, shopping, and parties with my workmates when we had days off. It was out of a sense of novelty, which I no longer have. I am in love with someone. Before there were no male workers on the same production line with me. All skilled workers were male. I never thought I would fall in love with someone, as this factory had so few male workers that it was jokingly referred to as a "nunnery" by some.

When workers make mistakes, our forewoman gets angry, but there is nothing she can do except warn us that she could "give us a fine." But when workers are working too slowly or something, she might scold them with words like "You're too stupid! Go away!" But this rarely happens.

There are also college graduates working on my production line. I heard that it was not easy even for them to find a job. They do not differ from us. Some people may have easy tasks and those who have connections with management always get the easiest job.

Counseling Institutions and Recreation Facilities in the Factory

a. *Counseling and Psychological Service*: In order to help workers manage stress, a psychological counseling room was set up. It is a consulting office with only one part-time psychological consultant. Calling ahead for an appointment is required. The consultant is from outside the firm, and only comes for appointments. The factory pays the fee. I think they are advertising one thing and doing another. The consultant asks workers to pour out their feelings by offering an emotional outlet, but provides no substantially effective solution. Workers who go there are asked their department, name, and other information. Issues brought up in the consultation, if relevant to the factory, can be reported to the management. However, very few people go, because no wants to recognize his/her own psychological problems. I know only one of my hometown friends who has been there.

b. *Dormitory Service Department*: Issues related to dormitories can be reported to this department. For instance, staff there help quarreling roommates to resolve issues or help them switch rooms. Workers can also report if there is no hot water or something is lost. They offer dorm supplies such as trashcans and brooms for free and some simple sports equipment like ping pong balls and shuttlecocks. They also provide room keys if you lose yours. Staff there are nice and enthusiastic.

c. *Residential environment*: The factory offers living accommodations. Each floor of the dorm has twenty-four rooms with seven people in each room. The building is new, equipped with toilets, balconies, and fans. The top floor, the eighth one, now has air-conditioners, after workers complained several times about the heat. The canteen is good and clean. Some workers, on average one for each floor, could afford a computer. However, it is too costly to set up Internet access individually and the factory declined to resolve this issue, though workers have complained a lot. Once a male worker even angrily threw away his computer.[2]

d. *Recreation areas*: Recreational facilities are provided by the factory, including a skating rink, basketball courts, badminton fields, table tennis courts, billiards, cyber cafes (the price dropped from 2–2.5 yuan to 1–1.5 yuan for one hour), and so on.

On New Year's Day and other festivals, the factory holds parties. One athletic competition is held every year. It was held on November 21 this year.

---

2. Editors' note: The reason for the worker throwing away his computer is unclear in the original. But it appears as if he may have been angry because he could not get Internet access.

Employee Meetings

Employee meetings are held on the fifteenth of every month; each department meets as a unit. The floor I belong to has about three thousand workers, and the foremen choose people to attend the meetings. Sometimes, they just randomly select someone. But some foremen would not ask people to go since they are afraid of causing production delays. I do not know when the policy started. I didn't attend any meetings until this year.

Some high-ranking managers attend these meetings (for example, the manager of the human resources office), as well as department managers, and floor assistants whose job is to recruit workers to each department and report workers' complaints to management. Each time only twenty to thirty workers (less than one tenth of the total employees) attend the meetings. Workers are asked in the meetings about their dissatisfactions and suggestions for improvement, which would be documented by HR managers.

These meetings can be effective, since some problems did get solved afterwards. Many issues were raised in the meetings, for example, lack of water, insufficient number of toilets, exhaustion from standing at work, and so on. Previously there were only toilets on one side of the shop floor, and this was totally insufficient. But after workers reported the problem, now both sides of the shop floor have toilets. Around 2003 and 2004, it was reported that standing at work was too exhausting, and therefore a batch of chairs were ordered for our shop floor. But later these chairs were all removed after an industrial injury happened when a girl fell asleep during work and her head hit one of the molding machines. We used to have work boots, but they were taken away since the shoe cabinet took up space on the shop floor (management was concerned about the extra expense). For any problem that might cost more money to solve, the factory owner often made all sorts of excuses, unless a lot of people complained. Recently, I suggested that they set up Internet access, but was declined. Their excuse was that some people got defrauded online so it is not safe. Though the management verbally agreed to "help apply" for the service, the actual implementation depends on "senior management."

Process of the Strike

Main Cause of the Strike

The factory did not increase salaries as mandated by the upward adjustment of the minimum wage. Typically, salaries were adjusted in July every year. In 2007, the city was late to announce the new minimum wage rate. The company had promised to raise the base pay a long time before. But when August's wages were paid in September, there was no pay increase. The general production line workers only earned around 1,500 yuan with no meals covered. So there was almost nothing left after paying for room and board, while the cost of living kept rising. Since the wage level in this company was somewhat higher than the neighboring factories, the cost of living in this area was also higher. Everyone was very angry with the inflation and the delay of the wage increase. Thus, the largest scale strike since 1959 broke out on September 12, 2007.

Walking Out

The strike took place shortly after I entered the factory—I was still simple, active, and playful. I participated simply because others were striking. The strike started in department B, which was the key department producing auto motors, and they received steady orders. There were around five thousand workers in this department, making it the most crucial place in the whole factory. The department had a five-floor workshop, and workers on the second floor of the workshop initiated the strike. It was said that the husband of the team leader on that floor had connections with organized crime, so she was willing to take the lead. Information about the strike was transmitted by text message among hometown friends, who were mainly from Henan and Hubei Provinces.

I was working the night shift on September 12. A rumor began to spread that workers on the day shift were on strike (though actually they were not), and that workers on the night shift should also go on strike. The general sentiment was to join. I was on the third floor and heard rumors flying around: "Workers on the fourth floor went on strike too!"

We were already unfocused and working slowly while talking about the strike. Suddenly, a girl cast aside a product she was working on, took off her gloves, and then threw them away. This inspired others to leave the shop floor in succession. The girl had worked here for a long time and was regarded as a brave and reliable workmate and as someone with a sense of propriety when speaking and handling various matters. She had her own thoughts and style and didn't just repeat whatever she heard elsewhere.

The products were usually sent out the day after production. Once the strike started, the reputation of the factory owner would be immediately damaged since they would lose customers and would have to pay a lot of compensation. So in order to avoid a strike the manager called all basic-level managers to a meeting. A Malaysian manager tried to appease workers, saying, "I'm begging you for help. Please no more strikes. I will be fired by the boss if you don't resume work, since this is my first time working in China."

The team leaders returned to the assembly line and pressured the workers. A supervisor came to the shop floor and warned, "Resume work now or go back home." Some team leaders treated workers badly in the hope of getting promoted. Workers felt outraged and directly left the workshops. The manager then asked the security guards to lock the exit and not let workers out. But a few security guards let some workers go. Security guards were directly hired by the factory and their wage level would follow any possible rise of wages for general workers. However, the security guard who was at the gate when I tried to leave was very rude, using his arms to try to block us in—and when he couldn't hold us back anymore, he tried to hit us. But as soon as someone shouted, "The security guard is beating us!" he did not dare to block us anymore. We immediately raced downstairs and more and more people followed. Several departments locked their doors so their workers would not run out and influence others. We went to the lawn and realized the strike had been planned beforehand. People were singing and dancing, albeit not well. Moreover, most people were in no mood to appreciate this entertainment during the strike. But some hooted. Workers on the other floors were also affected and came downstairs.

Sit-down and Highway Blockage

The next day (September 13), many armed police and officials from different government departments showed up. A loudspeaker blared with the voices of cadres from the municipal labor union saying that the strike was illegal and that workers must go back to work. One worker demanded there should be a wage increase. The union cadres asked how much of an increase, and the worker gave a number. A cadre replied that the present minimum wage standard had already been met in this factory and thus there was no possibility of a big wage increase. I was in the crowd and also complained a lot with my workmates. I said the wage was too low for me to send any money back home. Someone who came with the union staff glared at me and motioned to me to shut up. I was cowed and went away. But so many people were complaining; I was not alone.

That night, we continued the strike and staged a sit-down on the lawn. Then we walked around and someone proposed to go to the national highway. People walked out and I just followed them. It was around 10 p.m. Security guards were not able to stop us and had to open the gate. At that time, the big furniture store next to the factory happened to be celebrating its grand opening with a lot of colorful flags on display. I mentioned that they looked nice and someone pulled one out and brought it to me. Others liked this and snagged the rest of the flags.

At first, it was hard to block the highway since the cars were driving so fast. However, eventually more and more workers jammed the highway. Female workers stood hand-in-hand in the front, with more and more latecomers standing behind. We totally ignored the blaring horns. Team leaders and technical workers also participated in blocking the road. We didn't even recognize all of the people in the group.

After five or six minutes of blocking the road, the armed police of the local government arrived to drive us out. One ferocious officer corralled workers like ducks with a long bamboo pole, forcing us to the side of the road and grabbing the employee identification cards of those who resisted. The blockaders were mainly female workers who were easily frightened and didn't dare go toe to toe with them. The security guards stood hand-in-hand and pushed us off the road. One terrible security guard warned us to either go back or stay put. One male worker ran to the overpass and said, "If you don't let us strike, I'm going to jump!" But this sounded like a joke and did not receive any attention. At that time, we participated in the strike because it was fun. As the government prevented us from blocking the road, we then went back to the lawn inside the factory compound to hang out. The managers pressured the team leaders to gather the workers under their supervision. The team leaders chose to turn a blind eye to their own production line workers who had run off. We were tired of working and they were also tired of managing.

Wage Increase and the Resumption of Work

On the third day (the fourteenth), the boss offered a 30 yuan increase, which would increase the base pay from 750 to 780 yuan. He also offered to retroactively compensate the difference in base wages and overtime pay for July and August. Since the beginning of the strike, labor union staff and the factory boss asked us for our demands, but there was no consensus on wage demands. We had no idea how much the wage should be increased. We were only pursuing psychological consolation. One terrible team leader whose assembly line workers didn't go on strike was later promoted to supervisor by the Malaysian manager (the general manager in my department), rewarded for his arrogance, arbitrariness, insistence on opposing the strike, and for successfully intimidating the workers under his control. We strikers resumed work after getting this symbolic wage increase and seeing that some of our colleagues were still working. Soon the whole shop floor restored production. The factory demanded that we sign a letter of commitment to not strike again, and paid each of us 50 yuan.

After returning to the production line, we obediently stayed there but didn't do a thing. Hands were moving on the assembly lines, but no production was actually accomplished. Supervisors were moving around observing us, but I wouldn't do anything unless they were looking at me. While they were usually crude and aggressive, now they were all smiles. According to the old Chinese saying, "Requests with a smiling face should not be declined." They wanted to shame us into working. In order to show that she was taking her job seriously, our team leader intentionally shouted at me when high-ranking managers and the general supervisor stopped by. She felt that I was not obedient enough. I immediately replied, "I've had enough. Why do you only pick on me when so many people refuse to work?" The general supervisor asked me to go out with him after hearing my response. My workmates on the line were all concerned that I would be fired. Since I was young and always ready to help them, they felt worried for me. I said, "Let them fire me. I don't want to work here anyway." Looking very serious, the general supervisor asked me why we went on strike. I responded directly, "I was working on the assembly line; I could only work when products were passed to me! Since the others stopped, I had to stop." The supervisor had to change his style and said to me softly, "We all work away from home for others. We have no difference except the specific tasks. This stalemate is unnecessary. We will all suffer if the boss knows we are on strike." I said nothing and he had to let me go back to work. I was still unsatisfied, but had no choice. We continued with the slow-down. Later that night, they wouldn't let us go to the canteen but rather had the food served to us on the shop floor. Management was worried that if we left the shop floor, we wouldn't go back. Some workers ate, while others refused, feeling that "if I don't eat your food, at least I won't be guilty if I don't work." The next day the team leader began to demand higher output, and production was gradually restored.

Improving Benefits, Eliminating "Troublemakers"

Not only was our base pay increased, but shop floor management also improved. The factory set up complaint boxes for the workers and internal employee relation groups were established for workers to communicate with management. Managers were not as terrible as before. Each dorm was newly equipped with water heaters. A committee on occupational safety was established to conduct a monthly safety review, to distribute protective equipment, and to oversee production safety. The second day after the strike, some workers were called into a meeting with management. A female worker on our floor was fired because someone snitched her out as a leader. I thought that girl was really gentle, and that she didn't have any influence or seem like a leader. All of the workers from an assembly line on the second floor quit. Most of these workers had not wanted to continue working and were prepared to resign long before. They were the only ones unwilling to resume work and who demanded more when other workers had already returned to work. As a result, they "got permission to leave" or were fired. Some workers said management thought those workers were the strike leaders and so fired them all.

Personal Reflections

This is a large factory with a lot of workers. One has to rely on personal connections to get a promotion. Some positions are only open to insiders. There was only one time that the factory openly invited applications for the position of quality supervisors, and more than two hundred workers applied. In 2009, I worked as a team leader for a while, but soon returned to production work. I was not able to do it. To be a team leader, you need to have management skills and personal connections. Otherwise, when you have to work around the clock to fulfill an order, other assembly line leaders will not send workers to help you. Getting a promotion is based not just on personal ability, but also the right opportunity. For instance, one time the boss's daughter came to visit the factory. She asked a female worker to direct her to the bathroom and thought that the worker had a good attitude. As a result, the worker was given a promotion.

With respect to the strike, I knew so little that I had no idea except to follow others. If a strike happens now, I will not be afraid because I know some laws and will not be easily deceived. I also became confident enough to organize and communicate with others, and at least provide some suggestions. After the strike, I am content with my wage level, which after all is higher than in other factories in the area. My father also told me to be obedient. So after we got a raise I've continued to work here.

"Employee suggestion box. Please mention any issues except wage increases."

Chapter Fifteen

A Strike Demanding
Pay Increases in 2010

Interview conducted July 10, 2010

Factory Background

N Factory is located in one of the industrial parks in the outer zone of Shenzhen.[1] It is a watch factory, one of the so-called "three-plus-one" enterprises.[2] It was cofounded by A and B Companies. Our interviewee Z is from A Company, but the strike was waged by the workers in B Company. Therefore, the information collected in this article is mostly secondhand instead of direct experience.

The A Company only employs general workers, line managers, and team foremen. Other employees, including technical workers, supervisors, and higher-level management are all hired by B Company. The majority of the employees in B Company are college graduates. To recruit new workers, A Company usually posted job ads at the factory gate, while B Company went to the formal job fairs. Workers from A Company are assigned to every workshop on all floors. You can tell

---

1. Editors' note: In addition to its various districts, Shenzhen is divided into two "zones." The inner zone (*guannei*) is the area originally designated as a special economic zone, and it developed earlier. Beginning in the 1990s, most industry began to move to the outer zone (*guanwai*) and beyond.
2. Editors' note: "three plus one" (*sanlaiyibu*) refers to a type of enterprise common in Guangdong in which an overseas partner provides materials, designs, and machinery in exchange for processed goods.

which company someone works for by the color of their employee ID: white for A Company and red for B Company.

N Factory has three buildings in total and each has three floors. Workers in Building 1 produce watch casings. Z works on an assembly line producing coils on the third floor of Building 2. Building 3 is for quality inspection.

Wages and Benefits

The base pay for a general worker is 1,050 yuan per month, higher than the minimum wage standard in Shenzhen (900 yuan). Overtime compensation is calculated according to the labor law. The factory does not provide free room and board. Workers have to pay 37 yuan per month for a bed in a dorm room with ten beds, but usually there are seven to eight people in a room. Hot water is 18 yuan per cubic meter. Total expenses, including utilities, are about 50 yuan per month. There is a canteen in the living area. Each meal costs around 2.5 yuan. Z usually only had lunch in the canteen, which cost her about 100 yuan per month. She had breakfast and dinner elsewhere.

The Relationship Between Workers and Management

Z had worked in the factory before, but she felt the management improved substantially when she returned. For instance, she was hard up for cash when she entered the factory again and the line manager voluntarily lent money to her. Z initially attempted to borrow money from her previous line manager, but the current line manager told her not to be a stranger and gladly lent money to her. Z heard that the factory had a rule that allowed the boss to deduct money from the wages of employees to pay back line managers if they lent money to new employees. But Z was not clear about the details.

The relationship among general workers is relatively good. 90 percent of the workers on Z's shop floor are from Guangdong Province, but the majority of them speak Mandarin. They do not talk much at work. The room in the dorm is shared by workers from different workshops and a mix of day-shift and night-shift workers. When asked if there are any fights when one roommate disturbs another's sleep, Z said that it barely happened since everyone was considerate and consciously avoided disturbing others.

Married workers all moved out from the dorms to rent apartments.

Promotion

From low to high, the various positions in the factory are: general workers, line managers, team foremen, supervisors, managers, and general supervisors. If a general worker does well, he or she can be promoted to "assistant line manager" who is next in line to take over the line manager's position. Assistant line managers earn 100 yuan more than general workers. They will not replace line managers unless the latter leave. Z told us that she knew a female worker who had worked as an assistant line manager for about seven years until she quit the factory in 2009, since she never got a shot at a promotion.

Turnover Rate

Since N Factory paid higher wages and provided better benefits compared to the neighboring factories, the turnover rate was low. But that began to change this year. Z said that because of this the factory had been recruiting new workers from the beginning of the year until the day before the strike. She had started working at the factory together with more than thirty workmates, but now only a dozen or so remained. Some people quit after only a few days. The reasons for leaving varied. For instance, some veteran workers chose to quit because they wanted to go back home to get married. New workers quit because "it was too noisy on the shop floor" or "it was too exhausting to stand at work." Z also felt puzzled why the turnover rate was much lower previously, because at that time workers also had to bear the noise and stand at work. Quitting at this factory is easy; it's not like in other factories where managers will try to make it impossible. Z mentioned that managers would permit workers to quit as long as they worked for at least seven days. The rule is that you must submit a resignation application seven days in advance and the factory will not reject it.

Changes in the Factory

Z first entered the factory in March 2007 and later quit in February 2008. She joined the factory again on April 29, 2010. When comparing her two stints, she felt the there had been changes in the following three aspects.

Hiring

The first time Z was hired at the factory she had to pass an exam, but not the second time. In 2007 they were very strict about ID verification (fake ID cards were not allowed), medical tests, and other exams. Z came with more than forty applicants, but only around thirty people were hired. The second time was not as strict as before, since there was no longer an exam. They discriminated against applicants from certain regions, though Z couldn't say which regions in particular. But she mentioned that the girl she came with to apply for this job was immediately rejected once the recruiter found out she was from Guizhou Province.[3]

Discipline

Z felt that discipline was much stricter than before, which was manifested in some details. For instance, the time granted to workers for bathroom breaks was cut from 15 to 10 minutes, as was the afternoon rest period.

Living accommodations

Disinfection was conducted every half a month before, but now it was extended to every twenty days. Meals offered in the canteen were clearly worse than before, in spite of a price increase from 1.8 to 2.5 yuan per meal. However, Z thought this was normal given rising prices in general.

Causes of the Strike

Workers in B Company started to feel discontent with their pay after Foxconn and Honda increased their wages. But according to Z, wages in B Company were already much higher than hers were in A

---

3. Editors' note: Guizhou is one of the poorest provinces in China and has a large proportion of ethnic minorities.

Company. She complained that while technical workers earned on average 5,000 to 6,000 yuan per month and her supervisor in the coil department earned 10,000 yuan, new general workers only got paid 1,600 yuan. Even veteran workers were only paid 2,000 yuan. The pay gap was not due to different wage standards, but because the veteran workers had priority for overtime work. Typically, veteran workers were granted overtime work on Sundays, while the overtime schedule for new workers depended on orders. They were assigned overtime work only during busy seasons. If they didn't get overtime, they just got the time off.

The Process of the Strike

Workers in B Company went on strike starting Monday, June 6. They demanded a 60 percent wage increase. That same day, some journalists came to conduct interviews. Z initially thought the strike had already ended by Tuesday because workers had overtime work until 7:50 p.m. on Monday night. However, when Z went to the shop floor on Tuesday, she found workers in B Company all gathered in Building 1, since the majority of workers in that building worked for B Company. Z intended to participate in the strike, but others around her did not move. Her workmates were just whispering, but no one dared to join. Although the supervisor left, the team foreman and line managers were still on the shop floor monitoring workers, and the security guards were still downstairs.

Z chatted with workmates on the shop floor, and everyone complained about how timid the team foreman was. They felt he was selfish because a few days ago the supervisor asked him if he wanted to go on strike and he declined. If the current supervisor got fired, then he might have a chance to get promoted.

All of the workers in B Company went out on strike on Wednesday, but the team foreman did not allow general workers in A Company to leave the shop floor. The line manager warned workers not to leave, since he would not take the responsibility if anything unexpected happened. Some veteran workers couldn't bear to go against him since they felt he was a good person. The others did not dare strike, mainly because they were afraid that they might lose their employee identification card if they left their work post without permission. Having their employee identification card revoked itself would not result in being fined or fired, but they wouldn't be able to punch in. In normal times, only supervisors could get their card back and retroactively document their attendance. But Z felt that supervisors would not allow the same thing to happen more than three times. Nevertheless, Z had no idea what would follow if the card was revoked more than three times. She guessed that it might affect certain scores that are directly linked with their salary.

On Thursday afternoon, the factory gave two days off to all general workers, in order to keep them from participating in the strike. Many of them got permission to leave and went back home.

We asked Z whether general workers would go on strike if the base pay in N Factory didn't surpass the Shenzhen minimum wage standard (1,100 yuan) after July 1. She felt it was not very likely for them to go on strike, simply because workers were relatively content with the factory. In this industrial park, workers in N Factory like Z were regarded as well paid, since their base wage was already 150 yuan higher than the local minimum wage.[4] Z also mentioned many benefits, such as a two-month wage bonus for every full year workers stayed. There are more benefits at the end of year too. The turnover rate in N Factory is relatively low. Z gave us an example: "One worker from Hong Kong has worked here for a long time; he has been here since before I was born."

According to Z, B Company may increase wages for its workers after the strike, but A Company will not. On June 14, it was said that the base pay for general workers in A Company increased to 1,050 yuan per month, but we do not know whether B Company adjusted its wage level after the strike.

---

4. Editors' note: This appears to be inconsistent with the earlier statement. This, however, is an accurate translation of the original.

"Inflation" (cartoon from Mexico)

Postscript

Things change quickly in China. The stories in this book were collected in 2010–11, and many of the strikes that workers described took place in years prior. A lot can happen in China in a few years, and indeed there have been major occurrences in labor politics. While we cannot provide a comprehensive update, a few points are worth emphasizing.

First, worker unrest continues to expand. The absolute number of strikes and other forms of direct action remains high after a major surge during the 2008–09 economic crisis. Major legislative and symbolic efforts from the central government have thus far failed to tame worker insurgency. Unrest has appeared not just in the traditional manufacturing sector but also among transport workers, teachers, street cleaners, retail workers, and white-collar workers. What's more, strikes have spread from traditional hotbeds like the Pearl and Yangtze River Deltas to interior provinces. As capital has moved west to try to escape higher costs, worker resistance has followed.

As really dynamic growth has shifted into the interior of China, areas discussed in this book are already experiencing deindustrialization. Many highly labor-intensive firms in places like Shenzhen and Dongguan have closed up shop as a result of rising costs for labor and land. Local governments in these areas are less interested in retaining these low-end manufacturers and want to attract capital intensive, high-value-added production. Thus, while 2010 saw the growth of offensive or interest-based demands among one segment of the Pearl River Delta's working class, other segments have been thrown out of work. This has led to an upsurge in protests over severance compensation and unpaid wages. We can witness in today's China a major acceleration of the processes of industrialization and deindustrialization.

Even if a segment of workers in Guangdong Province are on the defensive, workers in this region have not given up their leading role in advancing labor struggles. The huge strike that took place at the Yue Yuen shoe factory, the world's largest athletic shoe manufacturer, in spring 2014 was a major event for a number of reasons. First, the scale was unprecedented, with a majority of the forty thousand workers in the factory taking part. But more important was that their central demand was for the employer to address years of unpaid pensions (as is legally required). This was significant because it demonstrated a maturation of worker demands beyond just wages. Many of the employees had been at Yue Yuen for ten years or more. As some workers were in their mid-forties, the question of social insurance became more important. Yue Yuen appears to have catalyzed greater attention to this issue. But resolving such problems will inevitably move beyond the workplace, as social insurance is directly related to China's spatially stratified citizenship regime that relegates migrants to an inferior status in the cities. Thus, there is a possibility that this cycle of protest may become more politicized.

Some readers may have wondered why there was no discussion of the more politicized protest among state sectors workers that took place in the early 2000s. After a flurry of media and scholarly attention more than a decade ago, workers from the state sector have largely dropped out of the limelight. But this does not mean that these workers have been acquiescent in the face of privatization and precariatization. The year 2009 saw major uprisings among steel workers in Tonghua and Linzhou. In 2011, workers at a Sinopec subsidiary oilfield in Henan went on strike over wage issues. And in 2012, workers in the FAW-GM Hongta Automobile factory in Yunnan Province struck over concerns about the selling off of state assets. While these are just a few examples, they suggest that struggles among the "old" working class in the state sector continue, even if the protests are not as large, frequent, or spectacular as in the early 2000s. As an increasing share of the state sector workforce is temporary and contingent, these sorts of issues will likely persist.

Another phenomenon that we have witnessed in Yue Yuen as well as other strikes is the increasing involvement of students, intellectuals, and allies in civil society. Labor and Marxist reading groups have proliferated on Chinese campuses in recent years. While we should not overstate the quantity, there are certainly a significant number of students who have gotten involved in labor activism, many of them going to work in factories. Since 2011 there has also been a proliferation of writing and analysis of labor politics within the country. This has been facilitated by new online forums such as WeChat (*Weixin*) and Weibo (a Twitter-like platform), but it has taken place offline too.

The best example of substantive student-worker solidarity took place in late summer to fall in 2014. In August of that year, nearly two hundred street cleaners at the Guangzhou Higher Education Mega-Center (a university "city" developed jointly by ten universities) struck over severance terms, as their employment switched from one subcontractor to another. While the grievances and method of resistance parallel those in many other strikes, several conditions aligned to stimulate a broad response from students. Proximity to the students, of course, was a factor. The workers had developed strong relationships and a ten-year history of struggles rooted in their previous displacement from land taken over to develop the MegaCenter, and they were also able to skillfully utilize democratic decision-making to resist divide-and-conquer tactics from the employers. Their confidence meant they could welcome student engagement without sacrificing self-direction. Students raised the call for solidarity (the earliest posting was reportedly read by three hundred thousand people), and organized teams to supply material and moral support. Dozens of students from half a dozen universities brought food, distributed bulletins, gathered petition signatures, and helped with media outreach. Risking reprisal from both state and academic authorities, this was certainly the most significant instance of student involvement in worker strikes in recent years.

There are also a number of examples where NGOs have become

more directly involved in strikes. This is, in our view, not an unalloyed good, as NGOs have no democratic basis on which to represent workers. In some cases, NGOs try to contain struggle to the legal terrain, thereby restricting the development of the workers' movement. Nonetheless, their advice can sometimes be instrumentally useful in the course of strike activities, and this appears to be happening with greater regularity.

On the other hand, many things have stayed the same. Local government interests are still tightly aligned with the interests of capital. Workers who cause too much of a disturbance are likely to face police repression. The official union remains antidemocratic and largely ineffectual, despite overtures toward an expansion of collective negotiations. At the national level, Xi Jinping has fostered an unbelievably repressive and hypernationalist political environment. And capital remains highly mobile—indeed, during the course of the Yue Yuen strike, Adidas announced it would be shifting orders to Vietnam. The challenges to constructing a politicized and organized worker movement in China should not be understated.

Despite these obstacles, workers in China continue to walk off the job every day. Books like this one can play an important role in the transmission of knowledge that is crucial to building a movement. Those of us outside of China would do well to take inspiration from the world's largest and most restive working class.